Running
Start

Running Start:

How to get a job in tech, keep that job, and thrive

Edited by Tenyia Lee.

Cover design and typesetting by Vanessa Mendozzi.

ISBN ebook: 978-0-578-38740-6

ISBN Paperback: 978-0-578-29844-3

ISBN Hardcover: 978-0-578-38739-0

Published by Alex Karp.

www.alexkarp.net

ALEX KARP

Running
Start

How to GET A JOB IN TECH,
keep that job, and thrive

Foreword by Pariss Chandler

BOSTON | INDEPENDENTLY PUBLISHED | 2022

"I believe that the best learning process of any kind of craft is just to look at the work of others."

— WOLE SOYINKA

CONTENTS

Foreword

My name is Pariss Chandler, I'm Founder & CEO of Black Tech Pipeline, and creator of the hashtag, movement, and community #BlackTechTwitter. For the past five years, I've worked in technology as a software engineer and technical recruiter. Today, my work and mission revolve around the recruitment and retainment of Black technologists.

I remember being new to the industry and being intimidated by the amount of work it took to break in and then progress in my career. The job hunt, preparing for interviews, and learning how to thrive in the workplace felt like climbing a confusing tree full of various branches I needed to research in order to make it in tech. I wished that there was one place that I could go to for answers. As someone who now works with candidates in all stages of their career and coming from all walks of life, I know that others would benefit from a resource of that nature as well.

Running Start is exactly that. This book centralizes and answers the rarely addressed questions about breaking into tech as a software engineer. How often are we told to "Google it," but still we struggle to find the exact answers to our questions? Not so with this book. Alex places himself into the shoes of a tech newbie and breaks down the trials, errors, and curiosities of how to apply to the right jobs, prepare for coding interviews, and thrive in the workplace. Even better, the information and insight provided in this book can be applied to your entire career, from entering tech to climbing the seniority ladder.

Alex's experiences and observations, and his advocacy work in getting underestimated technologists opportunities in tech, makes him the perfect person to publish such a necessary book. Alex has excelled in his career throughout the past 8 years. He began his career as a software engineer at companies like Wayfair and Microsoft, before progressing into an Engineering Manager role at Twitter. Alex has been involved in changing processes and creating initiatives that would positively, and equitably, impact his teams and workplace. For many leaders, it becomes difficult to remember what it was like as a fresh face to a booming, fast-paced industry. Alex, however, keeps those fresh, eager faces in mind and wants to continue to give back by offering valuable, important knowledge to give everyone their chance and a running start.

— Pariss

Introduction

Learning how to develop software is not easy. You've spent hours, weeks, months, years learning to code, honing your skills, building up a strong portfolio, and now you're ready to get out there. Right? Not quite. That was just the first step. Now you not only have to get a job, but you also have to keep that job. How do you get your foot in the door? How do you make sure you land somewhere you enjoy working, that will make all that hard work worth it? And what do you do once you're there?

My first job as a software engineer was full of self-doubt and worry, fed by a mixture of my own imposter syndrome and a manager that wasn't particularly interested in my growth. I spent a year in a constant state of anxiety and panic because of it and, in hindsight, it definitely held me back. After I got out of there, I had to un-learn certain things. Did you know that daily standups aren't usually an hour long and people don't usually bring their laptops to meetings out of boredom? Or that managers can help guide your growth, even if it's not directly under them? I had to learn how to seek out mentors and chart the path of my own career. I also had to learn how to ask for help.

As I've grown as an engineer and as I've become an engineering manager, I've realized that it doesn't have to be that way. You don't have to figure out how to navigate the job search on your own. Nor do you have to immediately know everything about your job when you start. And you certainly don't have to leave your career in the hands of others. These things don't get taught in colleges nor bootcamps. We don't talk about them enough as a tech community either.

As hard as it is for any of us to navigate the job market and really thriving in one's career, it's 100 times harder for anyone who isn't a part of the overrepresented majority — young, white, cis-gendered males with CS degrees who works on side project in their spare time (bonus points if he has a beard). This means that for anyone who is Black, Latinx, Indigenous, or Southeast Asian; a woman, transgender, or non-binary; a bootcamp grad, someone without a college degree, or a career switcher; a parent, a caregiver, or someone jumping into tech in their 50s; autistic, disabled, or different from the stereotype in any number of other ways, thriving in tech is just a little (or a lot) harder than it ought to be. You'll see me refer to this group as non-stereotypical engineers, because I think it's a wider group than we traditionally think of as "underrepresented minorities." This book is written for everyone, but especially for them.

A lot of other books out there seem to assume that all readers are the same, which can make them not as helpful to people who aren't. What many people (authors and tech recruiters alike) fail to see is that experience can come from various places, and that all are valid and valuable. If you've got years of leadership, communication, and teamwork experience, regardless of whether it's from a Fortune 500 company or your local church group, shouldn't you highlight that as something that sets you apart from the other applicants? Where other books might teach you how to fit in with the dominant culture in tech, I encourage you to focus instead of what you can add to these teams and companies.

I don't want the difficulty of your journey to be determined by the color of your skin or whether you have a good manager or mentor. I want you to be able to learn from my experiences and my mistakes so that you have the biggest possible advantage. I want you to have the resources and advice needed to really thrive in your career.

My hope is that this book will give you a running start as you're just getting into tech, and that it is a book you can come back to for years to come. I recommend reading it through the first time and then using it as a reference later on, revisiting relevant sections when you get to the next step in your job search or a new phase in your career. The end-of-chapter recaps can be especially useful for this. Use them on your first read to remind yourself what you just read, and if you're coming back to the book later on, as a quick refresher of each chapter's advice.

Now let's jump right in!

PART ONE

GETTING A JOB

CHAPTER ONE

The Preparation Stage

"By failing to prepare, you're preparing to fail."

— Benjamin Franklin

So you've learned how to develop software and now you're looking for a job as an engineer! While you're welcome to start applying to a bunch of companies right off the bat, a bit of preparation will go a long way. From making connections to figuring out what kind of job you want and what type of company you want to work for to tailoring your resume, there is a lot that you can do to make the whole application and interviewing process go smoothly for yourself. The more you prepare, the more likely you are to land a job that you love working on something that you're passionate about every day.

TIME IS A LUXURY

Preparation takes time. So does applying for jobs. Even if you're juggling a busy schedule, you should try to set aside some time for preparation to help you get the most out of the time you'll inevitably spend on applications. Any time you spend in this preparation stage will save you time in the long run because it will help you to focus on the opportunities that excite you most. Even if you can't do everything covered in this chapter, anything you can do will help.

SOUL-SEARCHING

Software engineering is a broad field. It's a *really* broad field. One of my favorite things about it is that there is probably an intersection between software and any interest you have, be it music, business, food, or just about anything else. But that breadth is a double-edged sword — having so many choices can be overwhelming. And that's not even considering the other vectors of choice you have in this job hunt.

So how do you figure out what jobs you want and what companies you want to apply to? Here is a set of questions to ask yourself to help point you in the right direction:

What fields interest you?

The best jobs are those that you're passionate about. What are you personally interested in? Your interests could be technical (e.g., mobile development, machine learning) or topical (e.g., travel, writing, sports, physics). Do some research and find companies that are doing those things and in those spaces.

What kind of software do you want to develop?

Some people want to develop business-facing software, like customer relationship management, finance, HR, and point-of-sale systems. Others prefer working on consumer-facing software, like e-commerce, social media, games, and health and wellness. When I was young, I saw software as a way to solve problems — usually my own problems, because I'm a bit selfish. But because of that, I tend to gravitate toward companies working on products that I either use or could see myself using. What kinds of problems do you want to solve?

Here are some additional breakdowns to consider when deciding what sort of software you want to develop:

- **Disciplines:** Backend, Frontend, Mobile, AI, Blockchain, etc.
- **Platforms:** Web, iOS, Android, Mac, Windows, etc.
- **Areas of Focus:** Infrastructure, Developer Tools, Product Development, etc.
- **Speed of Development:** Continuous deployment, frequent releases (every one to four weeks), infrequent releases (every two to three years), etc.
- **Other:** Programming languages, frameworks, technologies, etc.

What kind of a company do you want to work for?

Do you want for the structure and security of a big, established company? Or the speed and close-knit culture of a small, scrappy startup? Do you want to work at a company where everyone is remote? Or maybe one where everyone goes into the office every day? While these are all important things to think about, you should try to stay open to companies, jobs, and opportunities that you maybe wouldn't consider your first choice. It's entirely possible you'll get your first software job and love it, but it's very common for it to take a few different job experiences to really understand what you want. So, think about the questions above, but don't put too much pressure on yourself to have it all figured out right now.

NETWORKING

There are a lot of reasons why networking is beneficial. But especially if you're trying to break into the software field, building a network can open up opportunities. The more people you connect with, the more potential doors you can open. These doors can lead to things like job referrals, mentorship, advice, and maybe even friendship. Building a strong network will also help you later in your career, whether you're looking for a new job or hiring a new engineer for your team. It can also be a great way of looking into many different career paths to get a feel for what you want.

So, you want to network. Now what?

Building your network from scratch will always be difficult. If you can, try to leverage the people you already know. This could be your family, your friends, or your teachers. If you already have some professional experience (even if it's not in the software field), try to leverage your existing network. This could include your current or past managers, mentors, coworkers, or professors. You never know who will be able to give you valuable advice or connect you with someone useful.

Chances are, you already have a bigger network than you think. Did you go to college? That's a network! Even if you didn't study CS. Did you learn to code through a bootcamp? That's another network. Even if you were self-taught, it's highly likely that you interacted with other developers as you learned, whether in-person or through online forums. That's a network too. Take advantage of these networks because it's incredibly useful to be able to learn from your peers. We'll even talk about that more in chapter nine.

In networking, just like in life, it's important that you go out of your way to meet people who don't look like you and who have different lived experiences. If you're a part of the overrepresented majority, it's going to be more difficult for you to do this. But that makes it all the more important that you expose yourself to different people and perspectives.

By this point, you're probably asking, *"Well how do I meet these people?"*

Here's a few suggestions:

Interact on Twitter
Twitter is a great place to meet other engineers (and I'm not just saying that because I work there). Whatever type of software development you're into, there's probably a community on Twitter around it. Start following people! Comment, retweet, interact. If that community doesn't do a good job of including non-stereotypical engineers, make sure to look beyond that community. Following a diverse group of developers is an amazing way to broaden both your network and your horizons.

Meetups / Other Local Events
Maybe your local developer community has a regular Meetup you can attend. These are usually free events and can be pretty low-key.

(And they might even serve refreshments!) Some of them use a lecture-based format, some allow you to just bring whatever you're working on and work alongside others, and others do different things entirely. No matter what the format is though, there will always be time for networking. And since a lot of the people who attend these events do so on a regular basis, you'll likely have multiple opportunities to make connections with people.

Conferences

You get to spend a day or more listening to great talks, and there's tons of time to network. I know a lot of people — myself included — who have made great friends at conferences. The downside? They're usually expensive. Between registration, accommodations, entertaining and other expenses, a conference can run you hundreds, sometimes even thousands of dollars — especially if there is travel involved. If you have the opportunity and the means to go to a conference though, I highly recommend it. They can be a great place to meet other developers. Try inviting people to have lunch/dinner with you while you're there, or go with a friend who can introduce you to their friends or break the ice with new people.

Whether you try these suggestions or choose to explore other avenues to see what's available in your communities, building your network is invaluable when it comes to looking for a job.

YOUR RESUME

Now that you have an idea of what positions you'd like to apply for, it's time to work on your resume.

The resume-writing stage is where a lot of people do themselves a real disservice. They focus solely on their technical strengths, or experiences they perceive as directly relevant to the job. For someone trying to break into tech (whether it's their first job ever or they're transitioning from another field) this isn't often going to be a lot. And while a slim resume is totally okay for an entry-level position, it doesn't really do much to help you stand out from the crowd.

It's important to think about what really sets you apart from the rest. This is an area where I think people who have had other jobs before switching to tech have a huge, often underplayed, advantage. Are you a great communicator? A master problem solver? Does your previous work experience give you a unique point of view? Maybe you used the software that the company creates at another job and can provide feedback from the user's perspective. In other words, think about what you bring to the table. Don't limit yourself to just technical skills. Communication, leadership, problem-solving, and teamwork are examples of things that make your resume stronger.

It takes a village to be a truly successful development team. You need people from different backgrounds, with different life experiences, different skillsets, different abilities and disabilities. The more diverse the team, the better the product they'll put out. I'd bet a million dollars on it. Many job applicants are so focused on trying to make themselves "fit the mold" that they lose sight of what makes them unique, what makes them memorable, and what makes them a valuable asset to the team/company.

Once you know what you want to emphasize, it's time to write your resume. Your resume should tell a story. Every word you choose and experience you include should be in service of the story you want to tell. The order in which you highlight your project, work, and educational experience should follow a narrative that shows your growth and learning in key areas over time. How you describe each experience should tie back to your story's takeaways. And last but not least, you should use straightforward language and layout features to make your resume and the key points of your story easy to digest. Do this and your resume is sure to stand out. All of these things will help your resume to stand out.

SIMPLE IS SCANNABLE

A lot of companies use software to scan the huge numbers of resumes they receive. If your resume is hard to scan, it's possible that your information will be misread or that the system might reject your resume altogether before anyone has even looked at it! When it comes to designing your resume, go for something nice, yet simple. Use straightforward headings that the scanning software will recognize. Even better, include key words from the job posting you're responding to. Save the fancy-looking stuff for your portfolio.

GETTING YOUR FOOT IN THE DOOR

Once you have your resume ready, it's time to start applying for jobs! Like I said above, if you want to start submitting your resume to every open position you see, go for it! In this section, I'm going to focus on how to use your network to not only help you identify jobs that could be a good fit, but also how to use your network to get your foot in the door.

Direct Connections

If you're looking at positions at particular companies, check to see if you know anyone that works there. They can be a real asset! The obvious benefit is that they can refer you, which guarantees that your resume won't get lost in the slush pile. But less obvious is their ability to help guide you through the process. Don't forget, they interviewed there too! Ask them about what it was like. And don't forget to ask them about what it's like to work there.

Casting a Wide Net

In addition to using your connections to directly target your choice companies, I would highly recommend asking for help on Twitter, LinkedIn, and wherever else you can think of. Let people know what kind of roles/companies you're looking for, or else you'll get a lot of stuff that you don't expect. In order to increase your reach, see if people you know are willing to help by posting or reposting your behalf. If you are engaged in a community on Twitter or in person, let them know that you're job hunting. Not only might others in your networks have ideas themselves, but they're often happy to retweet and let you take advantage of the connections of their followers. The more people that see your message, the greater your chances of finding something you're interested in.

As you identify interesting opportunities, don't be shy about asking for help from the people that suggested them. Ask for referrals, ask about the company, make a new connection, and don't forget to thank them!

If you do all of this, hopefully you'll have at least a handful of interesting leads on positions to apply for. In the next chapter, we'll talk about how to turn those leads into successful interviews and job offers.

RECAP
Here's what we covered in the first chapter:

Ask yourself some questions
Spend some time thinking about what interests you in of the wide and varied world of software development. What problems do you want to solve? What kinds of companies do you want to work for? And what languages and technologies do you want to use? These will guide you as you build out your network and decide what opportunities to pursue.

Build your network
Take advantage of the people and the networks you already have. Use their connections to make new connections of your own. At the same time, make an effort to meet people. A few options include online communities, local meetups, and industry conferences. Your network is not only important for finding a job but also for learning and growing as an engineer.

Craft your resume

Your resume should tell a story. Really think about what makes you stand out as a developer. The things that we often call "soft skills" (communication, writing, organization, mediation, etc.) are things that people often overlook, but really do help a candidate stand out. The same goes for any way you can add diversity to the team in terms of background, experience, viewpoints, etc.

Let the world know that you're looking

Use direct connections from your network to target specific companies that you're interested in. Ask these people lots of questions and get them to refer you. In addition, let the entire world know what you're looking for! Use your connections and communities to boost your reach. One of my absolute favorite things about Twitter is how communities rally around a person when they put themselves out there to ask for help. The same goes for communities in other platforms and places.

Again, ask questions, make connections, get those referrals. And with a little bit of luck, you'll end up with at least a handful of opportunities you find interesting and that are interested in you. Next, your goal will be to turn those into job offers!

CHAPTER TWO

The Interview Stage

*Clay can be dirt in the wrong hands
but clay can be art in the right hands.*

— Lupita Nyong'o

The best way to fail an interview is not to study. The second-best way to fail is *to study.*

You're damned if you do, damned if you don't. So, what do you do?

The answer lies somewhere in between the two. Some studying is obviously going to serve you well. But trying to study *absolutely everything* you might be asked in an interview will only make you burn out. The key is to study smarter, not harder. So, what exactly should you spend your time studying that will give you the most bang for your buck?

GETTING THE LAY OF THE LAND

When most people think about studying for interviews, they think about preparing for the technical portions. They think about data structures, algorithms, Big-O notation, CS fundamentals, and everything else an interviewer might throw at them. In other words, they think about studying *everything*. And that's completely logical. The idea is that if you prepare enough, you'll be ready to answer any question that might come your way. The interviewers will be so impressed that they'll offer you the job.

This fantasy is even reinforced by people in the tech community. I've attended conference talks where the audience has basically been given a laundry list of every framework and concept to study. Honestly, a lot of interviews are even set up in a way that reinforces this way of thinking too. If so much weight is placed on a candidate's ability to solve an arbitrary problem, then of course they're going to spend the bulk of their prep time studying for that.

We'll talk about what to do instead in just a minute when we talk about technical interviews. But first, there's some important reconnaissance you need to do to learn more about the interview process you'll be facing.

SOME PEOPLE JUST SUCK

While a majority of people will (hopefully) be rooting for you, it's very possible you'll run into a recruiter, interviewer, manager, or company that just isn't on your side. That should be a red flag. I once went through an interview where my interviewer sat there checking email on his phone the entire time. Your interview is as much of an interview for them as it is for you. If something makes you uncomfortable or if something seems wrong, go with your gut. It's better to find these red flags early on rather than finding them only after you've joined the company. For more on this, check out the interlude after this chapter.

"Ask and ye shall receive."

Chances are if you're going through the interview process, you're working with one of the company's recruiters. Here's a secret you might be surprising to learn: *Your recruiter wants you to succeed.*

No, really.

Why? A bunch of reasons, but most of all, they're incentivized to fill open positions as quickly as possible with the best candidates possible.

For you, this means that they're looking to help you show off the fullest of your abilities. Some recruiters will send you information upfront about what each portion of the interview will entail and what they're looking to see. If they don't, it's important that you ask for this information. Here is what you really want to know from them:

1. What will the interview process look like?
2. For each interview panel, what is the format and area of focus?
3. What skills or traits are the interviewers looking for? Interviewers call these "signals."

4. Overall, what is the hiring manager looking for in a solid candidate?

I guarantee you, asking those four questions will make a major difference in how well your interviews go and how you feel going into them. Because when it comes to studying, without this information, you are faced with so much more than you could ever hope to learn. These questions will help you narrow it down significantly.

You might be thinking, *"Can I really ask these questions? Isn't that cheating?"* Yes, you definitely should ask those questions. And no, it is absolutely not cheating. As I mentioned, a lot of recruiters will even tell you this without you asking. But if you're the one to bring it up, you'll receive one of three responses in general:

1. The worst possible outcome is that they refuse to give you details about the process and areas of focus. This is a huge red flag in my book. Any company that relies on secrecy and surprise as part of their interview process is fundamentally flawed. They're so afraid that someone will try to game the system that they turn their interview process into a nightmare that doesn't actually test your ability to do the job. Don't waste your time with them.

2. Next is the yellow flag outcome: In this scenario, they're not opposed to answering these questions, they just don't have much in the way of material prepared to give you a good answer. Really this means that they haven't spent enough (if any) time thinking about what they're really looking for to be able to focus their interview process on that. This might not cause me to pull out of the interview process, but it would definitely be on my mind the entire time. If you get this sort of vague response, try to see if the

recruiter can press the hiring manager for more specifics on what they're looking for in a candidate.

3. And finally, the best outcome is that they have the information compiled and are happy to share it with you. This shows you're dealing with a company that's being thoughtful about how they hire and interview. It also means that they're not relying on tricks and surprises as part of any potential weed-out process.

Hopefully it was scenario three and you were able to get a pretty good idea of what they're looking for and what they're going to be focusing on. This info will help you narrow down what you need to study. Even if you ended up in scenario two, you were hopefully able to get some idea of what they're looking for in a candidate and can prepare accordingly. If you ended up in scenario one, run.

Now we can study.

THE TECHNICAL INTERVIEWS

The most dreaded part of the interview process is hands down the technical interviews. At some companies, you might have as few as one or two interview sessions; others will put you through an entire day of technical interviews. It's honestly not even unheard of for companies to interview over multiple days. I'm not going to dive too deeply into some aspects of technical interviews because there are already so many resources out there on how to memorize algorithms and such. I'll mention a handful of them in the appendix. Instead, I want to focus on how you can hone your most important tool that will serve you through every interview — problem-solving. This is so important and yet almost no one thinks about it, so I'll say it again bold: **if you study only one thing, make it problem-solving.**

So many people focus on memorization for the simple reason that, like I mentioned above, we're so afraid of encountering a question that we don't know the answer to, and so we try to know the answer to *everything*. The problem? It's not possible to know everything. There will always be something you don't know.

In fact, some interviewers will keep pushing until you're in a situation where you don't know the answer. If you've ever had an interview where things just kept getting harder and harder, your interviewer was probably pushing you to see how far you could go. Usually, this is a good thing! It means you've performed beyond expectations. But it also happens to people who spend a lot of time memorizing types of problems. If you breeze through the main problem, they'll just make it harder.

Instead of trying to memorize every type of problem an interviewer could possibly throw at you, here is the three-step problem-solving framework I recommend using when approaching any technical interview problem.

Step One: Understand the Problem

The first step is to understand what's being asked of you. Interview questions are vague — often *deliberately* so. Start by repeating the problem back to the interviewer just to make sure you're both on the same page. Next, you'll want to ask clarifying questions. Here are some good ones to help you assess the task at hand:

- *"What assumptions should I be making?"*
- *"Is it a system with frequent input that needs to be time-efficient?"*
- *"Is storage space a concern?"*
- *"What types of input are valid?"*
- *"Am I allowed to use standard library functions or do I have to write everything from scratch?"*

By asking these questions, not only are you setting yourself up to succeed at solving that specific problem, you're demonstrating the skills needed to take a task, assess what you need to know in order to solve it, and ask questions to get that info. This is a valuable skill for an engineer and your ability to think this way will not go unnoticed by your interviewer.

The next thing you'll want to do is understand the logic that you'll need to implement. The best way to do that is to try to work through the problem manually. Take the simplest input — often zero, one, or an empty array — and figure out the desired output. What's the simplest way you can get that desired output? Walk through it step by step. Then do the same thing with the next simplest input. And a third time, if needed.

The hope here is that as you go through this exercise, you'll start to see a logic develop that you can turn into code. Doing this is actually pretty similar to test-driven development.

Finally, it's important to think about what the exceptions might be to the logic you've developed. For an algorithm, this might mean asking yourself questions like *"What sets of inputs are invalid?"* or *"What sets of inputs produce non-standard results?"* If you're developing a piece of UI, you might ask instead, *"What happens if the user taps/clicks somewhere unexpected?"* or *"What happens if the user enters letters for their phone number?"* or *"What happens if the server returns an error or invalid data?"* Make sure your logic takes into account these exceptions as well.

PROPER PREPARATION PREVENTS POOR PERFORMANCE

By this point, you might be thinking, "When do I start actually *writing* the code?" This is normal. People get nervous during interviews. Their instinct is to get something down — anything. After all, something is better than nothing, right? Not necessarily.

Even though it might not feel like it, doing this initial setup work will save you time in the long run. Any decisions you make at this stage are "cheap" — that is, if you decide that you need to change something, it's quick and easy because you haven't spent any time writing out code yet. Once you start writing code, the closer you get to the end, the more "expensive" decisions get. At that point, removing sections of code, changing architectures or algorithms, or making any other adjustments to how you solve the problem can take a lot of time and rewriting.

Making solid decisions before you start writing code will pay off five-fold in terms of time spent actually writing.

Step Two: Plan and Prioritize

People tend to see these problems as whole tasks that need to be completed. Either you get the whole problem right or you don't. But that's not really the case. Often problems have many different sub-components to them and can be broken up into discreet chunks. If you can identify those sub-components, then you could reasonably start completing chunks of the work. And you could even test them to prove that they work. To me, a person who has only 60% of the problem solved but has several pieces that are actually working is more impressive than someone who is 90% of the way there but has nothing working to show for it.

Think of it as a test of your ability to break down large problems into smaller, actionable pieces. This is an important skill as an engineer and one that you'll use frequently. Why wouldn't you want to show it off?

Now that you've got the different pieces identified, it's time to prioritize them. This is like a sprint planning session. Only instead of planning the next two weeks, we're planning the next 30 minutes or so.

Here are some things to keep in mind as you prioritize:

- What pieces do you know how to implement?
- What pieces depend on other pieces?
- What are the most difficult pieces that could put you at risk of not finishing?

Now we have a plan! We are finally ready to start writing some code.

Step Three: Write Some Code

Like I mentioned in the previous step, you ought to complete at least *something*. Focus on working through the pieces of the problem one at a time. Get one piece done and use the momentum to work on the next piece. It is much better to get something working than to get to the end of your time having done a lot of planning but with nothing written.

A note of caution though: That cool new language that you've been picking up lately? The neat trick that you recently read about on Stack Overflow? Save them for another time. Now is not the time to try anything fancy or new — new languages or shortcuts are always trickier and more nuanced than we anticipate, and then if something goes wrong, it's harder to fix because we're not as familiar with what's going on. In an interview setting, stick to what you know.

As you complete each piece, take a moment to re-evaluate your priorities. Is the plan that you came up with still good? Or do you need to move things around? Maybe there was a piece that you didn't know you needed?

Congratulations are in order at this point! You've got a working solution. It may not be the prettiest or fanciest — in fact, it absolutely shouldn't be. If you have extra time at the end, that's when you can bring in the fancy stuff. That's the time to start thinking about things like implementation trade-offs, testing, and code structure. If you try to do it as you're working through the problem, you run the risk of trying to optimize too early, which could again leave you in a position where you end up with nothing working.

Like any other skill you might learn, problem-solving and interviewing take practice. When you're nervous, it's a lot harder to call upon a skill. By practicing these three steps of problem-solving, you greatly increase your odds of being able to focus on the problem and really shine.

Always Think Out Loud

I've got one last piece of advice when it comes to technical interviews. It might sound obvious, but this is important enough to call it out specifically: *You need to think out loud.*

Interviews are all about gathering data. As the interviewer, you're talking to someone you've probably never met before, trying to figure out if they have the skills that match the job they're applying for — all in the span of 30 minutes to an hour. This is incredibly hard to do.

As the person being interviewed, it is therefore in your best interest to make it as easy as possible for the interviewer to see your skills, to make them really shine. How do you do that? By thinking out loud!

Thinking out loud is a great idea for a few reasons. First, like I mentioned before, it helps the interviewer see and understand your thought process. Not only does this make it easier for them to identify the skills they're looking for, but it also makes them more likely to give you partial credit if you don't get to finish a problem or get it completely right. People mistakenly think that getting the right answer is the goal in a technical interview — it isn't. As an interviewer, I often couldn't care less about the right answer. I'm much more interested in how you got there. And if you're thinking out loud, it allows me to understand where you're going and how you got there. This means that if it seems like you are on the right track, I'm likely to give you credit for that.

THE BEHAVIORAL INTERVIEWS

"It's no use of talking unless people understand what you say."

— Zora Neale Hurston

Often, it's called something like a "cultural fit" interview. But I think that's a terrible way of looking at it. Calling it a "cultural fit" interview reinforces the idea that companies are looking for someone just like everyone else who already works there — that's the opposite of diversity. Your behavioral interview is just as much about what new skills and perspectives you bring to the table as it is about how well you "fit" the company's existing culture. And just like with your resume is the chance to tell your story, the behavioral interview is your chance to showcase what makes you, you! It is here that we focus on the human side of things.

What Interviewers Really Want to Hear

The biggest mistake people make during behavioral interviews is telling the interviewer what they think the interviewer wants to hear. They always tell stories where they're the hero. When asked about their weaknesses and opportunity areas, they either can't think of anything or they try to turn a weakness into something that sounds like a strength. Or worse, they say absolutely nothing of substance.

As an interviewer, I'm looking for certain signals that give me insight into a candidate. I've talked to a lot of interviewers across several companies, and here are some of the signals that they often say they're looking for:

Growth Mindset: How do you handle challenges? Do you like to learn new things? What do you do when presented with feedback? What have you learned from your previous experiences, failures, or mistakes?

Communication: How do you keep people up to date when you're working on a project? What happens if you don't think you're going to finish on time? How do you interact with people who are junior to you? your peers? those senior to you?

Self-Awareness: Do you know your strengths? Do you know your limitations and opportunity areas?

Coachability: How well do you handle suggestions from others? What do you do with constructive criticism? Do you seek out feedback?

Leadership: How do you build relationships with people? How do you help, unblock, or level up your teammates? How do you get others to buy into your ideas?

Humility: How do you handle making a mistake? How do you answer a question outside of your scope of knowledge? How do you treat people who are junior to you?

Collaboration: How do you work with groups of people? Is there a role you tend to play within a team? How do you distribute work fairly?

Notice that nowhere in there did I once mention anything specific to software development — that was intentional. If you have engineering stories that demonstrate these qualities, that's great! But if you don't (perhaps you've switched careers, or you're fresh out of school) that doesn't put you at a disadvantage. It just means that you have to present your prior experience in a way that demonstrates the skills and qualities that your interviewers are looking for.

This is your chance to shine! By highlighting these skills, even if they weren't gained at a tech company, you're helping the interviewer connect your prior experience to precisely what they're looking for.

What's your story?
The people who perform best on behavioral interviews are not the people who are amazing at everything and make no mistakes—no one is faultless, and I wouldn't believe you if you told me you were—they're the ones who have been the most introspective about their careers. Here are a few questions to ask yourself to help you do some honest self-reflection:

What makes you unique?
The best teams are those with the most diversity. What do you bring to the table? What about your skills/background/experience would be beneficial to the team/company?

What lessons have you learned throughout your career/ schooling/life?

What have you learned from your own mistakes? What have you learned from the mistakes of others? How has that influenced the way that you work? How have you handled those mistakes in the moment?

What are your strengths? What are your opportunity areas?

Think very carefully about these. Be as specific as possible. Also consider why you might choose to bring up specific strengths and opportunity areas during an interview.

Don't shy away from your own opportunity areas — no one's perfect and we all have room to grow and improve. What have you always wanted to be better at? What situations maybe make you uncomfortable and how do you confront them? What are some goals you've set for yourself? How have you tried to make progress toward them?

When you're thinking about your strengths, don't limit yourself to just tech-related strengths. Do you have any leadership experience? Have you displayed resilience in the face of adversity? Do you have any experience teaching or mentoring? All of these are examples of skills to highlight that can really set you apart from the rest of the applicants.

How to prepare

Now that you know what you want to focus on, it's time to prepare. You're going to want to have in your back pocket between three and five stories that highlight the things that make you unique, the things that make you awesome, and the things that make you an introspective human being. The stories should come from a wide range of situations, since this will help you answer as many different questions as possible.

In order for the interviewer to get as many of the signals that I mentioned above as possible, you want to make sure that the stories you choose are well-rounded. As such, at least one of these stories should likely be of a time where you are *not* the hero. Maybe even two of them. For these stories, you'll want to highlight what you've learned and how those lessons have influenced you.

The key to the "lessons learned" stories is balance. As an interviewer, I expect you to have made mistakes. However, I'm also going to expect you to have learned from them. The lessons learned should be equal to or greater than the mistake in scale. For example, if you had trouble remembering to do something, I'd expect to hear about what you do now to remind yourself of important tasks. If you had trouble communicating with someone, I'd expect to hear about how you worked on your communication skills. If you had a massive blowout argument with one of your coworkers, I'd expect to hear (a lot) about how that has influenced how you listen to others, resolve disagreements, escalate problems to your manager when necessary, etc. The bigger the problem, the bigger I would expect the resolution to be.

Once you have picked your stories, you need to practice explaining them clearly. You want to make sure that you cover all of the important parts while getting straight to the point. There are many different frameworks for how to do this, but I recommend a simple one like Situation-Action-Result (SAR). In this framework, you break up your stories into three sections. First, you give the interviewer context on the situation. Next, you describe the task that you needed to accomplish and what steps you took to get there. And finally, you talk about the impact of the work and how it relates to the interviewer's question.

Your interviewer will want to ask follow-up questions, so your answer needs to have enough details (or hooks) to give your interviewer something to work with. The key is to make sure your answer is elaborated enough for the interviewer to have follow-up questions but short enough to keep their attention.

You've probably heard about hooks as catchy openings to articles, books, and stories. They're what get readers interested.

Hooks in interview stories act similarly — they give the interviewer just enough information to pique their curiosity so that they ask about it later. When you're coming up with your stories, it's important to think about what follow up questions someone might ask. I would even recommend having someone else read them and come up with questions. Do you have answers to those questions? Do those answers contribute to the overarching narrative that you're trying to tell?

As an interviewer, I'm listening to these stories to get an understanding of the candidate's skills and experience. But it isn't always easy, depending on how the candidate tells the story. I have had candidates tell me stories to which I cannot for the life of me come up with a follow-up question. The easiest way to help your interviewer (or even to help direct your interviewer to something you want to draw their attention to) is by building in hooks.

ACING YOUR INTERVIEWS

It's interview day! You've spent time studying, self-reflecting, practicing problem-solving, and crafting stories, and now it's time to put it all to use. You're probably nervous, but that's okay.

Here is my golden rule of interviewing:

Prepare as best you can,
but expect everything to go wrong.

That's not to say that everything WILL go wrong, but I feel like this is still something that is really important to remember. Think of it like trying to stand on a moving train or bus. If you stand with your legs perfectly straight, expecting the whole ride to be smooth, you'll probably fall. But if you bend your legs slightly and acknowledge that there will be bumps along the way, your legs will be able to dampen the movement and you'll make it through the ride still standing.

Let's talk about some tips that will help you win the day and walk out of your interview feeling confident.

Get the Ball Rolling Early

Interviews are all about inertia; you might need to push yourself to get started, but it gets easier once the ball's rolling. Doing well in your first interview helps to build confidence that can help you in your next interview, and the one after that, and so on.

It's also important to note that at some companies, interviewers will actually pass on their feedback to the next interviewer. This creates bias and isn't done nearly as often nowadays, but I'd wager it still happens in some places. My interview at Microsoft was like that. I had five interview sessions and each one immediately emailed their feedback to the next interviewer. How do I know? I saw my fourth interviewer reading an email that said how well I was doing. Talk about a confidence boost!

But unfortunately, interviewers sharing notes this way can be a double-edged sword. If one of your interviews doesn't go so well, then your next interviewer will know about it. Hopefully they don't let that affect them, but it's really hard for it not to. It can also be hard for you to recover if you stumble or lose momentum. Whether it's your first interview of the day or somewhere in the middle, picking yourself up from a mistake or a not-so-great interview can be tough. But don't get nervous—your nerves are your own worst enemy during an interview. The thing to remember here is that you don't need to impress everyone to do well. In a well-designed interview, you're allowed to have strengths and weaknesses. They're just looking to see how you balance out. So don't count yourself out just because you had a hard time with one of the questions. Just try to nail the next one. It's still absolutely worth trying.

Pace Yourself

A full day of interviews is like a marathon, not a sprint. If you put all of your energy into the first interview, you'll start to get tired, anxious, and forgetful later on. It's much better to spread your energy evenly throughout the day. How do you do that? There are tons of different ways of keeping yourself calm, but one of my favorites is simply by taking deep breaths. Progressive muscle relaxation is another thing you could try if you have a few minutes between interviews. And make sure your basic needs are met: remember to eat, drink some water, take a bathroom break, etc. Whatever strategies you choose to manage your stress, make sure that you practice them ahead of time. Strategies only work if you can access them in moments of stress. If you're able to stay calm, you're much better able to regulate your energy and emotions, and you're much more likely to show your best side.

Reminders from an Interviewer

1. Your interviewer is hoping you'll succeed.
2. Everyone starts out with a clean slate.
3. You don't need to be perfect.
4. Practice helps build confidence.
5. Things won't go perfectly.
6. Your interview performance says nothing about you, who you are or your value.
7. True confidence in an interview comes from being able to solve problems that you don't already know (read: haven't memorized) the answer to.

ASKING QUESTIONS

Most companies and interviewers will try to leave five to ten minutes at the end of each interview session for you to ask questions. This is a valuable opportunity for you to gather information, so make the most of it by preparing some questions ahead of time. Don't forget that you're interviewing them just as much as they are interviewing you!

Back in chapter one, you did some thinking around what sort of company you are looking to work for. Start there. You should consider what you *don't* want in a company, team, or manager and direct your questions at searching out any red flags. If you've had experience in a few jobs, you'll probably have a good idea of what you're looking to avoid, but it might be difficult if this is going to be your first job. I would recommend coming up with a list of questions in advance; it's hard to remember what to ask when you're in the moment.

If you're looking for suggestions, here are some great questions to ask:

- What sorts of things are you looking for in a successful engineer?
- How are decisions made on this team and this company?
- What is the culture around taking vacations and working remotely?
- Why is this role important to the company?

- How does the team measure success?
- Is there anything that you think I should know about this role in order to make an informed decision?
- Is diversity important to this company? How do you try to attract and retain talent from a diverse range of backgrounds?
- What's the culture around team hierarchy? Do people tend to defer to what their manager or senior engineer tell them? Or are they encouraged to think critically and push back when it feels appropriate?
- What opportunities for growth are there in my role?
- What do you wish you could change about the company? What is the company doing to address that area of opportunity?

Asking well-informed questions signals to your interviewer that you are interested in the position. But more importantly, it helps you gather the data that you need in order to make an informed decision about your career and your future.

RECAP
Phew! We covered a lot of ground in this chapter. Let's go over it quickly as a reminder.

Getting the Lay of the Land
It's important to set yourself up for success. Ask questions of your recruiter to get a better idea of what you'll encounter during your interview. From there, the most important thing you can study is how to solve problems. Not specific problems, but problems in general.

The Technical Interviews
Problem-solving is the most important skill to have in your toolbox

during a technical interview. Use these three steps to solve any problem: (1) understand the problem, (2) plan and prioritize, and only then (3) write some code. Don't rush ahead to coding too early, and always think aloud! This structure should help you approach any problem you encounter, even when you don't know what to do.

The Behavioral Interviews

Focus on the narrative you're trying to tell about yourself and prepare stories ahead of time to find the best way to convey it to your interviewers. We talked about the different types of signals that your interviewer might be looking for and how to choose stories. We also learned about Situation-Action-Result as a framework to keep our stories brief without missing any of the details.

Acing Your Interviews

The golden rule of interviewing is: "Prepare the best you can, but expect everything will go wrong." Keeping that in mind can help you when things aren't going to plan. Getting the ball rolling early on can be a big help. And to keep the momentum going, stay relaxed and take time to care for your body and yourself throughout the long day.

Asking questions

It's important to ask questions at the end of your interview. Think in advance about what information you want to learn and what questions you might want to ask. I also shared a list of questions to get you started.

Once you've done your prep work, you should be ready to interview with confidence! Pretty soon, the offers will start pouring in. Head to the next chapter to learn how to choose between multiple offers and how to negotiate your fair value.

Bad Interviewers Exist

really hate that I have to include a section like this, but I think it's important that people know that there are bad interviewers out there. And unfortunately, the farther you are from the software engineer stereotype — young, white, cis-gendered male with a degree in CS from a well-known school — the more likely it is that you'll encounter these types of interviewers. Let's take a look at the various kinds of bad interviewers so you can know to recognize them if you find yourself sitting across from one.

First, there are the interviewers that are bad to everyone. These are the ones who have something more important to do than interviewing you. Or they like to use interviews as an opportunity to show off their "superior" intellect. Or they are bored and aren't paying attention to what you're saying.

Second, there are the interviewers that act like gatekeepers. These are the interviewers that are specifically trying to keep certain people out. I've heard stories of interviewers who would change their interview style based on the race of the candidate. If the was white, they would ask normal questions, provide support, and generally be a good, collaborative interviewer. But if the candidate was of a race that they thought represented an "affirmative action" hire, they would ask difficult questions, provide zero support, and really put the candidate through their paces. These interviewers don't see anything wrong with this. In fact, they think that they're doing their part to help "the people hurt by affirmative action." It's disgusting.

If you find yourself in a situation with an interviewer like this, there is honestly not a ton you can do in the moment. If you have the courage to call out your interviewer, that's awesome. But it takes a lot of nerve, self-confidence, and emotional energy to do something like that, and I don't blame anyone who wouldn't feel up to it. (I know that I certainly wouldn't have been able to do something like that when I first started looking for a job.) And often, if you try to call out the interviewer in these situations, they'll just double down on what they've been doing. So unless you feel prepared to deal with a defensive interviewer, I recommend just trying to do the best you can in that sucky situation.

Another thing that you can try is ending the interview. This really depends upon how you think things are going. If you feel like you're not being given a fair chance, and you don't think it is going to get any better, ending the interview early is a totally valid choice. You do not owe anyone your time, and there is no reason to waste it sitting there and putting yourself through an interview with an interviewer who isn't giving you a fair chance. This also takes a bit of courage, but I find that it's a lot easier to do now that we're in the age of virtual interviews. If you're interviewing in person, once you announce that you'd like to end your interview, the recruiter will usually come collect you. They might ask a few questions about your interview experience as they walk you out. In a virtual interview, it's even easier. Just let them know your decision and end the call. A recruiter might reach out to you later on to hear about your experience, but you're under no obligation to talk to them about it.

If you're looking for language on how to end an interview, try: "I'd like to end my interview here, please. I don't want to continue with the process." I'd recommend being as polite as possible, but in no circumstances are you required to be nice, to say you're sorry, or to cushion your words in any way.

One thing that people might worry about in confronting their interviewer or ending the interview early is the risk of appearing to be uncooperative, stubborn, or just straight up mean. But in reality, what you're doing is setting boundaries. You have the right to set boundaries around how people interact with you. You have the right to be given a fair interview. You have the right to protect yourself and your emotional well-being. And if a hiring manager or a company sees that boundary-setting as negative, that's a bad sign. People, teams, and companies should respect your boundaries. That's your right.

Can a bad interviewer tank your chances at getting an offer? Unfortunately, yes. In an ideal world, the team interviewing you has data from multiple sessions, and would be able to see your interview with the bad interviewer as an outlier. But that doesn't always happen. It's really up to the recruiter, the hiring manager, and the rest of the team to examine things critically and call out any unfairness.

But honestly? You don't want to be working at a place like that. I know that I say this with an immense amount of privilege — I have an established career as a software engineer, I have an emergency fund that allows me to focus on finding the right job and not just take the first offer I get, and I'm able to pass as someone who mostly meets the above stereotype — but I still think it's true. If you didn't get an offer because of a bad interviewer, it means that either everyone at the table shares that interviewer's views and thinks that's okay (which means that you could expect the exact same sort of behavior while working there), or they're not all like that but didn't notice that one of the interviewers was discriminating against you (which means that the team itself might not be gatekeeping, but they're also not doing a great job of thinking critically and being an active ally). Neither of these is a recipe for a happy work experience.

Now, I didn't just write this section to tell you that there is nothing you can do about bad interviewers. Nor did I write it to remind you that you don't want to be working at places that let bad interviewers be a part of the interview process. I wrote it because in situations like this, it's really easy to cast doubt upon yourself. Was that interviewer really ignoring me or did I just not keep them interested? Was my interviewer really giving me harder questions because I'm not white or are their interview questions just harder than I thought they would be?

When it comes down to it, I think it's important that we acknowledge this fact: bad interviewers exist. If something doesn't feel right to you, you're probably not imagining it. My advice at that point is to do your best to put it behind you, thank them for showing you their true colors in advance, and move on to your next opportunity.

In situations like this is, if you feel comfortable, let the recruiter know how you felt about the interview process. Hopefully they listen. But if they don't, that's their problem.

Anyway, that's enough talking about bad interviewers. Hopefully you never encounter one!

CHAPTER THREE

The Offer Stage

*"When choosing between two evils, I always like
to try the one I've never tried before."*

— Mae West

ongratulations! You got an offer! Take a moment to feel
really good about yourself — you deserve it! Your hard
work is finally paying off.

But the hard work isn't over quite yet. Whether you got one
offer or many, now it is time to decide which offer(s), if any, are
worth pursuing. And then there is the negotiation process. If that
sounds like a lot, just remember the bright side: Putting in a bit more
effort at this stage will help to ensure that you're at a company that
you love, where your needs are fulfilled, and where you're getting
paid your fair share.

And even brighter, the tables have now turned. Now that you know that one or more companies want to hire you, you're the one in control. In order to make the best choice, it's important that you make sure to evaluate each company as carefully as they've evaluated you.

In this chapter, I'm going to propose a framework for evaluating an offer. Whether you have multiple offers to consider or just one, it's important to evaluate any prospective employer with the same degree of scrutiny to make sure that their values and practices align with you and your needs.

NARROWING IT DOWN

There are a few different things to consider when deciding whether an offer is right for you:

What is the company culture?

Interviews can tell you a lot about a company's culture, if you ask a few questions and read between the lines a little bit. Based on what you saw and heard during your interview rounds, consider the following:

- How do decisions get made? From the top down, or bottom up? Who is consulted?
- Do the engineers have any say in what they work on? Do they often have to pivot on the whims of senior leaders?
- How do engineers interact with product managers, designers, QA, etc.? What is that give and take like? Is it pretty balanced or do product managers dominate the conversation?
- How self-aware is the company? Do they think that they have all of the answers and are doing everything perfectly, whether or not they actually are? Or do they admit that they have areas of improvement and then talk about what they're doing to work on them?

Obviously, a company is going to want to put its best foot forward in an effort to court you. This can lead them to try to put a positive spin on everything. But how well does the information you receive from your recruiter and the hiring manager match up with what you observed during your interviewers? What about what you find on websites like Glassdoor?

I believe that it's important for a company to be aware of its strengths and opportunity areas in order to improve. Make sure that you ask your interviewers what they wish they could change about their company. Follow it up by asking what their company is doing to improve in that area. Do they know the issue exists? Are they taking active steps to address it?

What is the team culture?

While a company will have an overall culture, the culture that you experience will vary from team to team. This is especially true at larger companies. So it is important to find out more about the culture of the specific team you would be working on.

What is their work/life balance like?

This is a tricky one, because you don't usually get a satisfying answer if you ask it directly. But some things to think about include: Do team members regularly work more than 40 hours a week? Are there parts of the year that are considered "crunch time" where people are expected to work longer hours? Are people actually encouraged to take PTO?

Is the team's culture "level based"?

It's important to remember that everyone, even a brand new engineer, can have good ideas and ask thoughtful questions, and has the right to be treated with the same respect as any senior member. Not all teams operate like this. Here are a few great questions to ask:

- What is the last thing you learned from a junior engineer?
- What is the most important thing you've ever learned from a junior engineer?
- Who does code reviews?

What is the makeup of the team?

There are a lot of different directions that this can go in, but a few things to consider are the types of engineers on the team, their levels, and their backgrounds. You don't have to be BFFs with your teammates, but it's absolutely worth making sure that you're at least comfortable with them.

Who will my manager be?

Not enough people think about this one. Make sure that you find out about your manager! Both from the people on the team and from the manager themselves. You're trying to figure out if your would-be manager is someone that you can work closely with. Here are some questions you can ask:

- *"What would you say is your management style?"*
- *"Who is the last person you promoted and what was that journey like?"*
- *"What is your performance management philosophy?"*

Hopefully these questions should help you figure out if you can work with your would-be manager. Does your manager feel like someone you could trust? Do they feel like someone who has your best interest at heart? Does the way they operate mesh with you and your working style?

Will I be happy?

Think back to the first chapter, where you did some soul searching. The goal was to figure out what sorts of opportunities would make you happiest. How does this role at this company compare with what you came up with before? It's okay if the role doesn't exactly match what you imagined, but it's important to evaluate whether the difference is okay with you.

Were there any red flags?

Think back to your interviews. Was there anything that anyone said or did that made you feel uncomfortable? Anything that struck you as odd? Did people avoid answering any questions that you brought up? Did you feel any pressure during the process to make a decision quickly? If you answered yes to any of those questions, think carefully about whether you want to move forward with that company.

But wait! I forgot to ask some of these questions...

Not to worry! At this stage, it's totally reasonable to ask if you can chat with your would-be manager and/or would-be teammates. You don't want to draw out this stage too long, but if you're still not sure about some of the things I mentioned above, it's completely worth it to take the time to get some answers. Companies will often be happy to schedule another conversation, as it's another opportunity to sell you on joining.

UNDERSTANDING YOUR OFFER

"Risk comes from not knowing what you're doing."

— Warren Buffett

Now that you've weeded out any companies that wouldn't be a good fit for you, it's time to evaluate the offers themselves. In order to do this, it would help to understand the different components of an offer.

Base Salary

Your base salary is the amount of money that you're guaranteed to be paid in a year. Base salary is the most stable component of your compensation package. It comes regularly (weekly, biweekly, monthly, etc.) and you can calculate exactly how much it will be. This number doesn't depend on performance — neither the company's nor your own. This is the number you should be using as you calculate your living expenses.

Bonuses

Bonus plans go by many different names and have different nuances to them, but they tend to follow the same general pattern.

Every X months/year, you'll get a bonus of between Y% and Z% of your salary, with a target of T%. This is determined by your own performance, the performance of the company, or a mixture of the two.

For simplicity, let's assume that the base salary is $100k and you receive a yearly bonus. Let's say that the bonus could be between 0% and 15% of your salary, with a target of 12%. If the bonus is just based on your own performance and you're meeting expectations for your role, then your expected bonus is roughly:

$$\$100,000 \times 12\% = \$12,000$$

But in reality, you could end up with anywhere between $0 and $15,000.

Things become more complex if any part of your bonus is based on company performance. It's a lot harder to estimate what your bonus will be without knowing how the company is performing. However, target percentages help you estimate your bonus. As long as your company performs as expected, you're likely to end up with that target percentage.

But because bonuses are by nature variable, it's a bit riskier to consider them as part of your yearly income.

Equity

Here's where things get even trickier. Equity is the riskiest part of your compensation package. It is entirely linked to the company's performance. If the company does well, you stand to gain. If the company does poorly, your equity could be worth very little. The idea with equity is to incentivize employees to help the company succeed — if some part of your compensation is based on how well the company does, it's in your best interest to make sure that the company does well. The problem is that it's often much more complicated than that. To further complicate matters, there are two different kinds of equity.

Stock Awards

These are the more straight-forward of the two. A stock award means that you are given a certain number of shares. These awards usually happen over the course of three to five years at certain intervals, called vests. With stock awards, you should look at a few things:

- **Vesting Cliff:** This is how long you have to wait before you receive your first chunk of stock. Historically, companies have gone with a one-year vesting cliff, but six months or even less is becoming more common.

- **Vesting Schedule:** This lets you know how much stock you'll receive and when you'll receive it. Here is an example of a vesting schedule. Let's assume that you start your new job on January 1, 2021. This means that you won't receive any stock for the first six months (the vesting cliff), but then you vest every 3 months after that. It's important to remember that if you leave the company for any reason, you forfeit any stock that has yet to vest. So in the example above, if you left in April 2022, then you would forfeit the 100 shares that would have vested in July 2022.

Vesting Date	Number of Shares
July 1, 2021	200
October 1, 2021	100
January 1, 2022	100
April 1, 2022	100
July 1, 2022	100

Stock Options

Stock options are more common at companies that have yet to go public. A stock option gives you the ability to buy a certain number of shares at a predetermined price once the company goes public. Generally, the earlier you join the company, the cheaper the price.

Stock options are pretty risky because they don't have much actual value until they're converted to stock.

I'm honestly not the best person to ask when it comes to understanding stock options, so I will include some helpful links in the appendix if you'd like to learn more.

Other Benefits

Salary, bonuses, and equity are the three biggest pieces of your offer package, but there are other benefits to consider as well. Things that could make a difference include 401k/retirement plan matching, tuition reimbursement, and employee stock purchase programs. Some companies even make payments toward your student loans! These are all things that could tip the balance when weighing an offer.

FIGURING OUT YOUR WORTH

"Life is a battle. You either enter it armed,
or you surrender immediately."

— Lorelai Gilmore I, *Gilmore Girls*

The last piece of information you'll need in order to enter negotiations prepared is your value. If you're looking for your first job or just entering the software field, it can be hard to have an idea of how much you should ask for. But even if you already have a job, how do you know that you're being paid enough? Regardless of your situation, it's smart to do a bit of research to figure out what your fair value is.

The myth that people shouldn't talk about their pay has been around for a long, long time. In fact, some companies go as far as putting that into people's contracts that they cannot share this information with others. Companies do this because they know that it is the best way to keep wages low. If you're not talking to your coworkers about pay, how are you going to know that you're getting paid 30% less than someone else in your same position with the same experience? While this can affect anyone, the people impacted most are women and BIPOCs — in short, anyone who doesn't fit the traditional stereotype.

This means that if you want to make sure that you're being paid fairly, you need to do research. It also means that if you're truly interested in helping to diversify the tech industry and making sure that everyone is getting paid fairly, you should add your compensation information to these resources. The resources are only as good as the data that people put into them — pay it forward.

Here are a few different resources that can give you an idea of what the market rate is for an engineer of your level in your city:

Glassdoor

Glassdoor is a website that collects pay information for a vast number of companies around the world. Employees at the very company you're considering might have volunteered their pay information on this site, where you can view it along with employees' reviews of their experiences working there. If you can't find any salary information for the company you're considering on Glassdoor, I recommend studying numbers from similar companies in your city to get an idea of what the market rate is.

Glassdoor also has a salary estimate feature based on your title, location, and years of experience. This is a nice tool for helping you visualize your potential salary at companies of various sizes, locations, etc. They even have a tool that "analyzes" your offer; just keep in mind that it seems to work better for more junior roles (I assume because it has more data points to go off of at that level).

Levels.fyi

Levels.fyi is similar to Glassdoor, but it's focused on compensation specifically at medium/large tech companies. If you're interested in seeing what Facebook/Google/Apple/Amazon pays for engineers in your area, it's a good resource.

Tech Salary Transparency Spreadsheet

This spreadsheet compiled by Taylor Pointdexter (@engineering_bae on Twitter) has thousands of entries from tech employees across a variety of levels, mostly centered around the US and Europe. You can find a link to the spreadsheet on the Running Start website. I highly recommend that you add your own pay info as well.

Use Your Network

In order to get to this point, you've hopefully built a network of at least a few people in tech. If you're comfortable asking, they might be able to shed valuable light on what fair compensation is in the industry or at a particular company. Especially if they're at the company that you're considering!

I would recommend getting compensation data from at least two different sources. And whatever resources you use, make sure that you get as many points of data as possible.

NEGOTIATING

"Everything is negotiable. Whether or not the negotiation is easy is another thing."

— Carrie Fisher

Now that you know how much to ask for, it's time to go to the negotiating table. Again, I don't want to try to reinvent the wheel. There are a bunch of resources out there on negotiation, and I'll include a list of them in the appendix. Instead, I'll focus here on a few specific pieces of advice that you may not find highlighted elsewhere.

Always Negotiate

Some companies will tell you that their offer is non-negotiable. This is almost always a lie. It's rare that a company is truly unwilling to negotiate on their offer. They've invested a lot of time and energy into sourcing and interviewing you, so they want you to join. Here are a few ways you can try to negotiate a "non-negotiable" offer:

Pick Your Battleground

It may be the case that they don't want to budge on the salary part of your offer. But don't forget that there are other parts of your compensation package too! Maybe you could get more equity, or a higher bonus target.

Signing Bonus?

Another option is to try to negotiate a signing bonus. Some companies will offer signing bonuses in the four or five figures (even six, in rare cases!) to get people to join. If you have to move for the job, they might be willing to give you a relocation stipend — another thing that can be negotiated.

Don't Forget About Other Benefits

People don't often think about negotiating for things outside of the compensation numbers, but if there is a benefit that you're really interested in, include it as part of your negotiation. Maybe you want the company to pay for you to attend X conferences per year. Or maybe you want more PTO days. If there is something that's important to you, let your recruiter know. You never know unless you ask!

Never Put Out the First Number

As part of the interview process, your recruiter is going to ask you for your compensation expectations. They might ask you straight out, or they might ask what you're currently making. Don't tell them. Throwing out the first number is the biggest mistake you could make. My favorite phrase for avoiding these conversations is this:

"I can't buy it AND sell it!"

Because that is exactly what happens if you throw a number out first: you're negotiating against yourself.

People getting their first job in tech can be especially impacted by this. It's often the case that the less certain a person is about what constitutes fair pay, the lower the number they throw out, the greater the chance that they'll be underpaid. As much as I'd like to say that companies will do the right thing and make sure that people are paid equitably, there is an overwhelming amount of data that suggests otherwise. Other things that you can say to not put yourself in this position include:

- *"I'd be interested to hear what the company had in mind in terms of compensation for this position."*
- *"I don't feel comfortable talking about my salary expectations until I've heard what the company is looking to pay for the role."*

Know When to Say Yes and When to Walk Away

You've done the research to figure out what is fair when it comes to pay and what the minimum amount is that you want. If they can't (or won't) meet your minimum, it's easy to know when to walk away. But if they're willing to meet or exceed your minimum, it's also important to know when to say yes. It may be tempting to try to optimize every aspect of your offer, but it's good to remember when you can stop negotiating.

Get Everything in Writing

This might seem obvious, but it's important enough that I want to bring it up. Make sure that whatever you agree to in your negotiations ends up in the final offer letter that you sign. Remember: an oral contract is only as good as the paper it's written on.

RECAP

In this chapter, we looked at how to evaluate, negotiate, and decide on offers from companies.

Deciding on an Offer

With any job offer you receive, make sure before responding that you have all of the information you need in order to make an informed decision. It might not always seem like it, but don't forget: you are interviewing them just as much as they are interviewing you. Find out about the culture of the company, the culture of the team, and whether you feel like you can work with your would-be manager. Never settle for a company that gives you a bad feeling or doesn't align with what you're looking for.

Understanding Your Offer

Salary, bonuses, and equity are the major three forms of compensation you'll receive. Make sure that you understand what parts of your compensation are fixed (like salary) and which are variable (like bonuses). Do the math to figure out what your total compensation would be for the first 2-3 years. There are also other benefits (401k matching, tuition reimbursement, PTO, etc.) that you'll want to consider as well.

Figuring Out Your Worth

How much are engineers in your area and in similar positions to yours getting paid? This is incredibly important because it's up to you to advocate for yourself, which means you need to be armed with knowledge of your fair worth.

Negotiating

Negotiation is a battle. Armed with the knowledge of what you're worth and what's considered fair, it's time to jump right into it. Often, a company will tell you that an offer is non-negotiable — they're lying. Negotiate anyways, but never against yourself; if you're being asked about your compensation expectations, ask for their number instead. You have to balance pushing to get what you want and accepting what you need. And it's not over until it's all in writing and you've signed the contract.

Now you can really celebrate! Hopefully this chapter has helped you figure out which offer you want to choose and how to get the best deal you can. In the next part of the book, I'll focus on how to hit the ground running as you start your new job.

PART TWO

HITTING THE GROUND RUNNING

CHAPTER FOUR

Your First 90 Days

"Words can come and go.
Your acts are going to speak for themselves."

– Javier Hernandez

You made it! You signed on an offer and now you're starting at your new job. Your first few days will probably revolve around onboarding: finding your way around the office, setting up your computer, and meeting your new team. But as the excitement starts to die down and you start to settle in, you might find yourself thinking, *"Now what should I do?"*

My answer to this question when I was at my first job was to have a panic attack at the end of my first week, leave work early, and drive home the three hours from Seattle to Portland crying. I don't recommend it. Instead, I hope you're able to use the insights that I've drawn from that experience to make the most of what can be a scary time.

For me, lists and plans helped immensely. The more preparation I put in, the more confident I felt at work. And don't get me wrong — preparation can certainly help. But what would have been even more helpful? Realizing that it was okay that I knew next to nothing about the technologies I was using. That it was expected for me to ask a million questions. And that it is normal to take three to six months (or even more) to ramp up and become a productive junior engineer.

So how do you get from here to there? Let's start with your first 1:1.

YOUR FIRST 1:1

Some people love 1:1s and some people hate them. While both feelings are valid, it's important to recognize 1:1s for what they are: all about **you**.

I tell the engineers on my team that 1:1s are our dedicated time to talk about them and whatever is on their mind. While that's true, it's also rather vague. What should you actually talk about? Here are some things to focus on in your first 1:1 with your new manager:

What should I be focusing on in the first couple of weeks? What about in the first 90 days?

These two questions are great because they help you understand what you should be working on right now, and where you should be heading. Some companies even do a 90-day performance review for new hires, so this really sets you up for success. These are questions that your manager should know the answer to and they should be able to explain your objectives clearly. And often, the expectations for you are much lower than what you might have built up in your head! The goal here is to combat anxiety with facts and knowledge.

If I have a question, how do you prefer I ask you?

I feel like this is an underrated question, especially for people in their first tech job. You're going to have questions — *a lot* of questions. So many questions that you'll worry about bothering your manager. By asking about this upfront and ahead of time, later you can focus on getting the answers you need and not worrying about whether you're annoying people. Asking this question helps you start your relationship with your manager on the right foot.

Will I be set up with a mentor on the team?

Hopefully you've already been set up with a mentor. But in case you haven't, it never hurts to ask! Having someone who is focused on helping you get up to speed is invaluable and can be the difference between hitting the ground running and crying under your desk — trust me.

How do you coach for growth?

Intentionality is the name of the game here. Would you like the first time you hear about your performance to be during your first performance review a year from now? Or would you rather hear about it on a monthly basis? By making your objectives for growth intentional and explicit, it helps to set clear expectations. And honestly, it'll probably impress your manager that you're thinking about these things. More on that later.

How often and for how long should we meet?

Never leave your first 1:1 without knowing when the next one will be. Cadence and duration are up to you and your manager. Personally, I would recommend meeting either weekly or biweekly, for 30 minutes or an hour.

Your first 1:1 should occur within the first two weeks of starting. If an initial 1:1 hasn't been set up by then, I would ask your manager about it.

You don't have to *like* your manager, but you do have to *work* with them.[1] And working together is easiest when you've developed a relationship. I'll sometimes spend a good half of the time or more of a 1:1 chatting about random, non-work-related things. What might seem like a waste of time actually helps the two of us feel more comfortable communicating with one another in general. I want the people on my team to be able to come to me with anything, and building rapport is how I do that.

Now that you've had your first 1:1, what else should you focus on?

---

1 While this is true in most cases, there are cases where you shouldn't feel obligated to work with your manager, such as if your manager makes you feel uncomfortable, if your manager violates your trust, or if your manager doesn't respect you or your work. In these cases, I would find someone to confide in (ideally on a different team), tell your manager's manager (if you feel comfortable), and talk to HR (they're hopefully trained to handle this sort of thing).

MAKE A GOOD FIRST IMPRESSION

For better or worse, first impressions are hard to change. This means that if you appear to be forgetful, standoffish, or dishonest at the start, people will remember that and it will take a lot of effort to get them to see you as anything else. The good news is that you can use this to your advantage! A little bit of work to make good impressions goes a long way here. In your first weeks, aim to:

- Meet as many of your co-workers as possible
- Speak up during meetings
- Communicate your progress frequently
- Take on a reasonable amount of work than you're confident you can accomplish

While this is good advice that can serve you always, it's particularly important during your first few weeks and months. If you establish a track record of engaging with your coworkers, asking questions, getting involved, under-promising and over-delivering, then you'll be off to a strong start. Notice how I didn't say that you should work long hours, get as much work done as quickly as you can, not ask for help from others, or teach yourself. Those are the things people usually think of, but they actually do much more harm than good.

ASK LOTS OF QUESTIONS

You might think that you should be cranking out code as soon as possible, but you'd be wrong. Your #1 job as a new-hire is to learn, and you do that by asking questions. Think about it — you're starting at a new job at a new company, with new people, and working within a new codebase. Even if you're familiar with the language and the frameworks, it is difficult to jump right into a new codebase and understand what is going on. *Where do you even begin?* That sounds like a question right there!

Assuming that you're jumping into a codebase that's more than a few months old, you're going to run into technical debt. You might see some really weird paradigms and odd ways of working around problems. Ask about those too!

Every time you ask a question, try to write down the answer — both for yourself and for others. Your company probably has some shared knowledge base (e.g. Confluence, Notion, OneNote, etc.), and you should make sure that the answer is written down there. Because if you have a question, it's highly likely that someone else starting out will have that same question too. It's very possible that a resource like this already exists, so don't be afraid to ask! Regardless, it's important for you to contribute to any FAQ document that already exists, or to start one if there is none, because not only are you getting the answer to your question, you're helping future engineers ramp up as quickly as possible. It's a really easy way of making an impact early on.

It's really tempting to rush through this phase and try to jump right into feeling established, but I think trying to ramp up too fast is a mistake. If you focus on how much code you've written and how many tasks you've completed, you're always going to feel behind. If you focus on learning and feeling comfortable with the codebase, then not only will you get the benefits of building that solid foundation, but you'll feel less stressed in your first weeks. It's counterintuitive, but sometimes you really need to slow down in order to speed up.

GETTING A MENTOR

As I mentioned above, having a mentor can be invaluable — especially in your first 90 days. The real value of a mentor is the individual attention that you receive. While your manager or your tech lead might have a handful of people or projects to focus on, your mentor is ideally focused solely on you and getting you up to speed. A mentor can help you navigate the team's processes and understand the codebase, and is a great person to ask all of the questions you've been encountering.

If your manager has not assigned you a mentor, make sure to ask them about it. If they are unable or unwilling to find you one, feel free to ask one of your teammates yourself! If no one is interested, I would consider that a red flag.

Here are some things that your mentor can help you with:

- Making sure that you're invited to all team meetings
- Helping you get your development environment set up
- Walking you through the process of merging/releasing code
- Understanding who to ask questions to and what the other teams do
- Navigating team/company processes and culture

When working with your mentor, it's helpful to think about how you learn best. Do you prefer to just dive in and get your hands dirty? Or do you learn best by watching first? Or maybe you love pair programming as a way of learning. Figure out what's most helpful to you and make sure your mentor knows that. You're already drinking from a fire hose; you may give yourself the advantage of learning in the way your brain works best.

And the most important thing to remember about your mentor is that they're there to help you succeed. If you look good, they look good. And if your mentor is any good, they'll actually care about you and your development. What does this mean? *Don't suffer in silence*. If you have a question, if you're feeling overwhelmed, if you need help, if you need *anything*, let your mentor know. The only thing that suffering in silence leads to is an anxiety attack.

NETWORKING, REDUX

You might have thought your networking days were over, but they've only just begun! I believe that there is a direct correlation between the number of people with whom you've developed working relationships and the amount of work you're able to get done. Developing relationships early on makes it a lot easier to go to a person later when you need their help. Not only will you know who to go to, but you'll feel comfortable going to them.

If you've been following along, you should already have at least two developing relationships — with your manager and your mentor. Now it's time to start meeting other people around the company. But how do you know who to meet? Again, just ask the question! Have your manager and your mentor each make lists of the people you should get to know. That's in addition to the people on your team, of course.

Now, to actually go and meet those people. There are a couple of strategies you can use from this point:

The Methodical Approach

The simplest way to go from here is to start working your way down the lists. Schedule to meet with each person, at a pace you feel comfortable with. That could be one or two a week, or even one or two a day! Try to mix it up a little bit — invite someone to get a coffee, or to lunch, or for a walk if it's a nice day. The possibilities are endless! And make sure to ask each person if there is anyone else they think you should meet.

The Popcorn Approach

If scheduling lots of these informal chats seems daunting, or if the lists you're given are super long, the popcorn approach might be better for you.

Pick one person on the list and schedule a chat with them. As we saw above, it doesn't have to be an awkward chat in a conference room. At the end of your chat, ask them who they think you should chat with next. Whomever they suggest, schedule a chat with that person next. Rinse and repeat.

Make sure to spend at least half of the time talking about things that aren't work-related. It might sound like slacking off, but learning about people's lives outside of work really is one of the best ways to develop relationships quickly and I can't recommend it enough. As you have these chats, hopefully you'll have fun, hopefully you'll get to know your coworkers, and hopefully you'll like all of them. But remember — just like with your manager and your mentor, you don't have to *like* them, but you do have to work with them.

RECAP

Your first 90 days are very important! But that doesn't mean that you need to stress out about them. Here are the things you should do to get the most out of your first 90 days:

Your First 1:1

Come prepared to your first 1:1 with questions and really take ownership over this time you spend talking with your manager. After all, it is all about you, right?

Make a Good First Impression

Making a great first impression doesn't have to be hard work. Listen, learn, and speak up. You'd be surprised at how far that gets you. But whatever you do, don't push yourself too hard. No one expects you to produce code immediately, and you'll get yourself stuck in a dangerous cycle that can only end in burnout. Your goal should be to work smarter, not harder. Right?

Ask Lots of Questions

Ask 1,000,000 questions. Okay, maybe not *literally* a million, but ask a lot. Ask like it's your job to ask — because it is! Asking questions helps you understand what's going on and develop a solid foundation. And if you write everything down, you're doing a favor to all the new hires who join after you!

Getting a Mentor

Hopefully your manager has already set you up with one, but you should go find one if they haven't! Your mentor can be an incredibly valuable asset in your first 90 days, and can be the difference between hitting the ground running and hitting the ground face-first.

Networking, Redux

Invite your coworkers to grab coffee, lunch, go for a walk, or whatever you or they like to do to meet as many people as possible. The more people you meet, the easier it will be to get things done in the long run.

And whatever you do, don't forget to enjoy this period. Stop and smell some roses! You'll be less stressed if you do.

CHAPTER FIVE

The Next 90 Days

"The first draft of anything is shit."

— Ernest Hemmingway

You're officially a veteran now. So why is it that you maybe don't feel like you know so much at this point? In fact, this is often the point where worry starts to set in. Everybody seems to stop talking about onboarding after the first 90 days, which gives us the false impression that we should be operating at full capacity on day 91. But that's almost never the case. Learning and ramping up are a continuous process, so it's totally okay if you're not feeling like a developer extraordinaire yet.

Let's talk about how to take advantage of these next 90 days to build on your success from the first 90.

BUILDING CONFIDENCE

By this point, you've talked to a whole bunch of people and you've poked around the codebase. It's likely you've also fixed a few bugs and maybe even started working on a project. That's a great start! Here are a few suggestions on how to continue building your confidence:

Keep a Work Log

If you're like me, it's nice to have something to look at when you wonder, *"What did I do today?"*

A work log is great because it lets you see how you've progressed from your first day. It's also helpful because when you're worrying about how little you've done, it can remind you of all that you have actually accomplished.

Not to mention, keeping track of what you've done is also incredibly useful when it comes time for performance reviews and promotions. As we'll talk about in the next chapter, you need to be your biggest advocate. As someone who has a hard time remembering what they had for breakfast, I highly recommend at least keeping a list of the projects you've worked on — this makes it a lot easier for you to advocate for yourself. In chapters 10 and 11, we'll look at how to use this information to get promoted and to find new opportunities.

When in Doubt, Ask!

Sometimes our brains are a little too good at trying to keep us safe by always looking ahead and filling that picture with worry. Particularly in situations like starting a new job, your brain raises the alarm that you're not learning fast enough. Or maybe you're not getting enough work done. Or maybe you're not making enough friends. Your brain knows that these are the things that you need to succeed in your new job. But that's where the trouble starts. You start to wonder *"Am I working hard enough?"* or *"Am I getting enough done?"* And left alone with your thoughts, what starts out as confidence erodes over time to become panic. Your brain is trying to keep you safe in the same way that it would try to keep you safe from a lion. And that's the problem.

So how do you break that cycle of doubt?

Ask! Ask your manager. Ask your mentor. Ask anyone you work with. Ask how they think you're doing or how they think you're ramping up. If you have someone on your team that you trust, tell them how you're feeling. Or even talk to a friend or partner about it! The worst thing you can do in situations like this is to try to keep your worries to yourself. Talk to others and you'll find that nine time out of ten, you have nothing to be anxious about.

Finding a Long-Term Mentor

In the previous chapter, we talked about finding a mentor for your first 90 days. Now it's time to embark on a relationship with a longer-term mentor. A long-term mentor should be chosen by you and be someone who can help you take your career where you want it to go. In order to figure out what you want in a mentor, start by asking yourself these questions:

- *"Where do I see myself in six months? A year? Three years?"*
- *"What do I want to learn how to do?"*
- *"What kind of support am I looking for?"*

Depending on your goals, a long-term mentor might be a more senior engineer, or a manager, or somebody else entirely. I have only one rule when it comes to choosing a long-term mentor: they shouldn't be part of your reporting structure. They shouldn't be on your same team, and they shouldn't be your manager or any of your manager's managers. Having a mentor outside of your management chain is important because it can sometimes be difficult to speak frankly about your thoughts and concerns to someone you report to directly. Enlisting a long-term mentor from a different team or even a different company helps ensure that you'll be able to get an outsider's perspective. But aside from that, your long-term mentor could be pretty much anyone. They could be:

- On a neighboring team
- From the company's mentorship program
- An acquaintance from a conference
- Someone you connected with online
- A coach through a paid service

For anyone who is interested in the paid service route, I include a few links in the appendix.

Last but not least, here is the biggest piece of advice I can give you at this stage to help you build your confidence:

Don't Compare Yourself Against Anyone Else.

It might sound counter-intuitive, but the anxiety you get from comparing yourself to others is never worth it. The real problem with measuring your success against others is that any comparison makes the assumption that too many things are equal. Things such as: the opportunities they have been given and the privileges they have, the amount of time they've put in, the speed at which they learn new things, and how well their skillset matches up with their work. It's also incredibly unfair to people who are parents, caregivers, disabled, struggling with their mental health, and basically anyone who can't (or doesn't want to) devote their entire life to working.

Comparing yourself to others assumes that everyone is the same, and that simply isn't true. Measuring your progress this way just sets you up to be unhappy and it's usually a replacement for thinking or asking about your opportunity areas. We'll cover what to do instead in chapters six and seven.

BUILDING RELATIONSHIPS AND TRUST

In your first 90 days, you spent a lot of time getting to know people. You put in extra effort to make a good first impression, and now it's time to build on that.

Meet Regularly with Others

Particularly for the people who aren't on your team and with whom you might not interact on a daily basis, it's important to make time to meet. I recommend setting up regular 1:1s with people to understand what they're working on, talk about what you're working on, and further develop rapport. If you meet and communicate regularly with people, it makes it much easier to reach out when you need something or when something is wrong.

These meetings don't need to be often or long. For most people, having these 1:1s every four to six weeks for 15-30 minutes is sufficient. If you're meeting with someone in person, it could be a good time to grab a cup of coffee and/or get out of the office.

Establish a Track Record

Particularly with the people on your team, it's important to establish a track record of delivering what you promise and communicating openly. Note that this doesn't mean that you have to work long hours or scramble to get projects finished. This is about taking small steps to build trust. How do we do this?

Under-Promise, Over-Deliver

In a perfect world, you would be so good at estimating your workload that you would able to deliver exactly what you've promised every time. You would be able to say *"I can complete that project in three days"* and it would be complete exactly three days later. But it doesn't always happen that way, even to the best of us. As a manager, I greatly prefer people finishing projects ahead of schedule instead of behind schedule. The best way to achieve this is to be completely honest with ourselves about what we can actually accomplish. Try to build in time for unexpected challenges. It's always better to give yourself too much time and delivery something early than to not give yourself enough time and let down your team.

TAKE CARE OF YOURSELF

Taking care of yourself is an **all the time** thing, but I think this is a key time to bring up its importance. During your first 90 days, you're likely too busy learning the ropes and meeting new people to think of much else. But during the next 90 is when you should really start to think about how best to set yourself up to flourish in the long-haul. How do you do that? Self-care!

Self-care is the practice of taking an active role in protecting your own well-being and happiness, in particular during periods of stress. Hopefully you have a team that cares about your well-being and happiness. But it's still important that you look out for yourself too.

Signs of Burnout

Self-care one of the few things standing between you and burnout. People in tech jobs are particularly susceptible to burnout, which makes it extremely important to know the signs and how to prevent it. What does burnout look like? It's feeling tired or drained most of the time, feeling a sense of failure or self-doubt, and a loss of motivation. It's a sense of detachment, feeling alone in the world, and an increasingly cynical and negative outlook.

Those are just a few examples. Keep in mind that burnout comes in many different flavors and levels. It can be caused by a combination of factors in your work and personal life. It can be caused by a specific project, team, or person. And depending on how long the stress continues and how bad it is, it can range from a small amount of stress to severe burnout.

If you're wondering how you can spot burnout, here are some questions that you can ask yourself: Does *every* day feel like a bad day? Does caring about my work or home life just seem like a waste of energy? Am I exhausted all of the time? Is a majority of my day spent doing tasks that are either mind-numbingly boring or overwhelming? Do I feel like nothing I do makes a difference or is appreciated?

But I think the easiest rule of thumb is: if you're wondering whether you might be burning out, you probably are. It's a lot more common than people think.

Recovering from Burnout

The amount of time that it takes to recover from burnout is highly dependent on how severe it is. It could take weeks, months, or even *years*! Some people recommend taking a break from working, if you can afford it. Here are some things you can do to help recover:

- Track your stress levels and identify your stressors
- Talk to a therapist and/or life coach
- Use your support network
- Speak up for yourself and ask for what you need
- Prioritize your work/life balance
- Do things that you enjoy
- Set boundaries

This is by no means an exhaustive list, but it's a good place to start!

Taking PTO

In addition to the strategies listed above, taking PTO is probably one of the most important things you can do for your career. Whether you're burnt out, on the path to burn out, or even if you're feeling perfectly fine, taking PTO is one of the best things you can do for yourself to help to regulate your stress and keep you performing at a high level.

Some companies give people a specific number of PTO days. Others have unlimited or "unaccrued" PTO, which means you can decide for yourself how much PTO is right for you. I tend to prefer the latter, but it only works if it's paired with a healthy company culture around taking PTO. Otherwise, it's just an excuse to make people too scared to take any vacation. If your company is in the unlimited PTO camp, I suggest talking with your manager to figure out what a reasonable amount of PTO looks like.

People are really bad at judging how much PTO they ought to take and are even worse about actually taking it. I've seen this become an issue especially during the COVID-19 pandemic, when people on my team wouldn't take PTO because there wasn't really anything they could do during lockdown besides stay at home. But when they did actually take some PTO, almost all of them still found it restorative. So as a manager, I like to work with each person on my team to establish the right amount of PTO for them.

The Rules of PTO

1. Do not compare the number of your PTO days with what others are taking. Different people have different needs, which is why PTO should be unique to each person.
2. Prepare for your PTO as best you can: Make sure that people are aware of your PTO, that there is a plan to keep your work moving forward if need be, and that you've written notes on the current state of your projects so that you know where to pick up when you return.
3. Unless there is a really good reason that you've discussed with your manager beforehand, you should turn off your email, Slack, and all other forms of work communication. If you've prepared properly for your PTO, everything else can wait.
4. Take PTO frequently. Some people like to save up their

PTO for a big vacation. But by doing that, they spend the rest of the year stressed out. Personally, I think that if you want to take a big vacation, you should do it! But you should *also* be taking PTO on a regular basis. I tell my teams that they should be taking at least one week of PTO per quarter and that's what I plan for in terms of team capacity.

PTO Doesn't Have to Be Expensive or Complicated

Sometimes taking time for yourself is not as easy as it sounds, even with PTO from your job. Not everyone can just pick up for two weeks and pamper themselves at a Tahitian resort. Nor does everyone have the luxury of being able to ignore their non-work responsibilities — children, elderly dependents, personal commitments, chores, etc. As much fun as it might be to get away from it all, taking fulfilling PTO doesn't have to be expensive or complicated.

Here are a few ideas for simple, smaller things to make the most of your PTO:

- If you have to stay at home, try spending time in a part of your house/apartment that you don't usually work in.
- Try going somewhere you don't usually go or have never been. It doesn't have to be far.
- If you have the ability, spend a night or two in a local hotel in a different part of town.

But most importantly, remember that PTO is one of your best tools to keep yourself happy, healthy, and performing your best. Be intentional about how you spend your time and make sure you have the proper plan set in place so that when your PTO comes around, all you have to do is focus on relaxing.

Other Types of Self-Care

Taking a vacation isn't the only way to care for yourself. Here are

some other important ways you should be watching out for your
well-being day to day:

Set clear boundaries

This one is hard. Our capitalist society does everything it can to
discourage us from setting boundaries. Don't believe me? Under
capitalism, our worth in society revolves around being useful — we
make it a moral issue. If you're useful, you deserve food and shelter.
Not useful? We'll begrudgingly hand you an unemployment check
or a social security check, but it won't be nearly enough money
to make ends meet, and then we'll look down upon you as lazy.
It doesn't matter whether it's temporary or permanent, whether
it's brought about by actual laziness or mental health, disability,
discrimination, unsafe working conditions, or some other circum-
stance. We'll look down upon you all the same. It's why health
care benefits are tied to your job — so that you only have access
to health care if you're a "productive member of society" and so
you're scared of losing your job.

In an ideal world, your manager and company would always act
in your best interest. But in reality, it's up to you to protect yourself
and your well-being. Setting boundaries is hard because you feel
like you're being difficult and unreasonable. But in reality, you're
usually not the one who is being unreasonable — they are. And
if they don't accept simple boundaries like "*I can't work on the
weekends,*" then that's not a healthy environment. See chapter 11
to learn more about when it might be time for a job change.

Set realistic expectations

A lot of developers, especially junior developers, feel the need to
prove that they can do things quickly, so they'll set unreasonable
expectations for themselves. They then either proceed to work 24/7
to complete the task by the deadline, or they don't make the date
and end up feeling like a failure. It's a no-win situation. Being a

good team member is all about setting the right expectations. If you think something is going to take you a week to do, say that. If it's going to take a month, say that too. Be prepared to explain why you think it'll take that long, but it's much better to set that expectation up front rather than having to deal with the reality later on of something not being complete by the time you promised to deliver it.

RECAP

Your first 90 days set you up for success, but your next 90 days and beyond should be focused on maintaining that success. Here's how we went about it.

Building Confidence

People tend to be their own worst enemy when it comes to confidence. Our brains are incredibly powerful but sometimes try to protect us from problems that we usually don't have anymore. In order to assure yourself that you are indeed on the right track, we can keep a work log, ask for feedback (which we'll cover more in chapter seven), and find ourselves a long-term mentor.

Building Relationships and Trust

Capitalize on the relationships you've already built and set out to build new ones. Grab coffee with coworkers, set up regular, brief 1:1s with people outside of your team. Trust is built slowly and steadily over time, so if you develop a track record of delivering on what you promise, trust will follow.

Taking Care of Yourself

This should go without saying, but you **need** to take care of yourself. Burnout is real and people who work in tech are particularly susceptible. Make sure to check in with yourself regularly on how you're doing, whether you're taking enough PTO, and speak up for what you need in order to thrive.

CHAPTER SIX

Using Your Manager

"The most common way people give up their power is by thinking they don't have any."

— Alice Walker

O ne of the biggest misconceptions that engineers have, especially at the start of their careers, is about the purpose of their manager. It's really easy to see your manager as a "puppet master," but you have a lot more agency in that dynamic than you think. And the people who I've seen grow the quickest are those who are able to use their managers effectively. "Using your manager" sounds like a horrible thing to do, but what I tell people is that they should look at me as a tool in their toolbox. There are a lot of things that I, as a manager, can do to help the people on my team grow and progress in their careers. I'll hopefully do some of these things proactively, but it is always valid for engineers to ask me to do them. We'll talk about what these things are below.

Every manager works in a different way, so let's talk first about understanding your manager's style.

IDENTIFYING YOUR MANAGER'S STYLE

This might come as a surprise, but there is no one way to be a good manager. Each manager will likely have their own unique blend of different management styles. None of these styles individually make for a good or bad manager. But it's still important to understand your manager's style, because that will help you work best with them and also help you use them most effectively. Here are some of the most common management styles:

Authoritarian

In an authoritarian system, decisions are made from the top down. Authoritarian leaders will decide not only what needs to be done but *how* it should be done, when and by whom. Managers with this style of leadership tend to create very structured and rigid environments. On the plus side, authoritarian leaders are good at making decisions quickly. They also make the chain of command very clear. On the negative side, people on these teams will likely feel untrusted and like their input doesn't matter. The team will also lose out on potential creative ideas and new learning from team members.

Visionary

Like the name implies, visionary leaders lead their team toward a vision. They'll set ambitious, long-term goals that will take the team forward. They will then use these ambitious goals to inspire their team to work toward them. In this case, only the destination is decided by the manager; it's up to the team to figure out how to get there. On the positive side, this allows the team to figure out for themselves the best way to achieve those goals, while the manager is still able to make long-term decisions quickly. On the negative side, having an ambitious goal thrust upon a team without much help from the manager can make the team feel resentful toward their demanding leader.

Transactional

Transactional leaders rely on rewards and punishments to get work done. If you do what your manager asks you to do, they'll reward you with a bonus or a promotion or some other perk. It's a simple exchange — you do a thing for your manager, and they do a thing for you. There doesn't need to be a long-term relationship between you and your manager, nor do you need to have a strong rapport. Transactional relationships can work well when it comes to managing teams of people doing work where very little creativity is required. incentivizing workers this way to do a lot to raise productivity. Unfortunately, teams with transactional leaders tend to have motivation problems (not everyone can be motivated by performance-based rewards), discourage creativity (you're only incentivized to do exactly what is being asked of you), and can have a pattern of low engagement (not getting a bonus or a reward if you're already struggling really piles it on).

Servant-Leader

Servant leadership is a bit of a buzzword, and many people who use the term don't quite understand what it actually means. At their core, a servant leader believes that leadership is the opportunity to serve others. Ideally, this means that they don't center themselves. They understand that even as the leader, they cannot take credit for the successes of a great team. They make sure that praise is deflected toward the people who actually did the work. And they try to get others to share ideas before they voice their own in an effort to take advantage of everyone's creativity and other strengths. By doing this, they share power and control with their team and are really able to get the most engagement and productivity out of them. The potential downsides of servant leadership are that it can take longer for decisions to get made, and some people might view a servant leader as weak compared to their opposite, an authoritarian leader.

Pacesetting

Pacesetting leaders are a bit like visionary leaders, but a bit more transactional. These managers will keep setting goals for the team to hit. They're the ones who will be working right alongside you to get these things done and wouldn't ask you to do anything they wouldn't do themselves. Pacesetting managers work well with highly motivated teams, but this leadership style can lead to team members burning out if people are not careful.

Democratic

Democratic leaders are all about making decisions together. Particularly when it comes to big, important decisions, these managers won't make a decision until they've heard every team member's opinion. They'll also work to get to a point where everyone agrees on a single decision before setting it in stone. On the positive side, democratic leaders really encourage their teams to think for themselves, share their own ideas, and take an ownership stake in the decisions that are being made. On the negative side, democracy takes a lot of time and hard work. If left unchecked, a democratic leader can spend so long trying to build consensus that they fail to make critical decisions quickly. An ideal democratic leader knows when to foster debate, when to try to get buy-in, and when there is enough buy-in on the team to feel comfortable moving forward.

Laissez-faire

These managers take a very hands-off approach to management. It's easy to think of laissez-faire leaders as lazy, but that's not usually the case. They place a lot of trust on their team to be able to make good decisions, finish projects on time, and ask for help when they need it. That last part is a key differentiator between a laissez-faire leader and lazy leader. Lazy managers want you to do everything yourself because they don't want to work. Laissez-faire managers want you to do as much as you can yourself because they trust and believe in you. These managers are the opposite of micromanagers. I've always been pleasantly surprised by how much people are able to do if you give them an ambitious task, encourage them to it, and then step out of the way — while being there to provide support if asked, of course. But that's the key: they will only jump in if they are asked to. They won't start offering advice unsolicited. Laissez-faire leadership works well with a team full of people who are driven and have good communication skills, but can be disastrous with people who have a hard time learning on the fly and who don't feel comfortable asking for help when they need it.

Your manager will most likely be a mixture of these leadership styles. For instance, I am a servant-leader at my core. But the way that I believe I can best serve my team is a mixture of visionary, democratic, and laissez-faire leadership.

Understanding your manager's style will help you understand what they value, how to work best with them, and how best to use them to your advantage.

IDENTIFYING AND ARRANGING OPPORTUNITIES

One incredibly helpful thing that your manager can do is to connect you with opportunities that will further your growth and your career. For instance, if your manager knows that you are interested in eventually moving into management yourself, they might set you up to mentor a summer intern, or help onboard the new person on the team. They might coach you on developing leadership skills or sign you up for training in preparation for becoming a manager.

The key to this, though, is that you need to make sure that you let your manager know where your interests lie. Hopefully your manager will ask these questions as part of their getting to know you and will follow up regularly to see how your interests change. If not, make sure that you let them know.

I like to ask people where they see themselves in six months, one year, three years, and 20 years. It might sound impossible to imagine yourself 20 years from now, and you might be wondering why that's a useful exercise at all. But you'd be surprised! For instance, you might want to be the CEO of a company, or a college professor, or even a rock star! (Do rock stars still even exist?) Regardless of whether your ideal role 20 years from now is on the same team, at the same company, in the same industry, or you may even want to be retired, there are skills and experiences that your manager might be able to help arrange that can lead you to your goals.

The shorter-term goals are generally easier for people to visualize. Like long-term goals, they help your manager identify opportunities for you and provide you with advice and coaching. But they're also useful for your manager to know because they might be able to point out if your short-term goals aren't setting you up for your long-term ones.

Regardless of how your manager does or doesn't ask about your future goals, make sure to let them know.

UNDERSTANDING YOUR PERFORMANCE

In chapter five, we talked about asking your manager or mentor about your performance, especially when you're not sure how you're doing. Your manager should hopefully be proactive about giving you feedback, and you're always welcome to ask. But there is more that you can use your manager for with regards to your performance than just regular evaluations. Here are some good things to ask your manager about:

The Career Ladder (or Jungle Gym)

In chapter nine, we'll talk about different career paths and levels. While I hope that will be informative in the general sense, the best way to learn about career advancement is to learn about the ladder that your specific company uses. Your company probably makes this information freely available — if they don't, run. But I think there is still value in going through it with your manager. The way that career ladders are written is often fairly vague. Management does this to try to support as many different roles and career paths as possible. While it's great that they don't have to create multiple ladders, the vague language can make it hard to understand what each level entails and how you're progressing toward the next rung. Here's where your manager comes in.

Promotions Process

If you're reading this as you're looking for your first job or as someone just starting out as an engineer, you might think that getting promoted is far, far away. But it's honestly closer than you think. At all of the companies that I've worked for, the general expectation is for a junior engineer to get promoted to mid-level within about 12-18 months. The best way to make sure that this happens, especially if you're aiming for the 12-month end of that spectrum, is to know exactly what it takes to get to the next level and what the process for promotion is.

It's easy to assume that if you focus on performing at the next level, then the promotion will take care of itself. But it's not always that simple. Some companies just defer to the manager — if your manager decides that you're ready to be promoted to the next level, then that's pretty much it — while others have arduous processes designed to force a manager to *prove* that you are performing at the next level before someone higher up approves your promotion.

Take a moment to ask your manager how promotions are handled at your company. Understanding the process allows you to set your own expectations as to when you'll get promoted. It will also let you know if there is any way that you can help move the process forward.

Getting Feedback from Others

It's really hard to ask people directly for feedback. And if you do, the feedback you receive will probably be generic. Sometimes this is because people feel awkward giving feedback directly to you.

Other times it's because they don't know what might be useful for you to hear, or there might even be a power dynamic at play that is getting in the way. This is where your manager can help facilitate. People are most likely to give open, honest, and actual feedback to a manager who asks about someone on their team than are to give that same feedback directly to a peer. Your manager should be collecting feedback for you regularly. This, in conjunction with their own observations, makes up the basis of the feedback and coaching that they give you. But it's possible that your manager might not be getting the full picture from the small group of people they are requesting feedback from. That's why it's important to make sure your manager is a) gathering feedback for you on a regular basis, and b) gathering feedback from the right people. If your manager has a more than 6 direct reports, it's possible that they might not have enough visibility into your day-to-day work to know who you have worked closely with. That's why it's important to let them know specifically whose feedback you think would be valuable.

We'll talk a lot more about feedback in the next chapter, so stay tuned.

SETTING AND ACHIEVING GOALS

Whether personal or professional, goals are an important thing to have if you wish to grow. But it can be hard to know what kinds of goals to set, and it can be even harder actually following through on them. Luckily, your manager is equipped to help you do just that! Some companies will explicitly ask you to write out your goals. Often, these goals are little more than completing the projects you have been assigned. I think that personal goals are really where the bread and butter is.

When I say personal, I don't mean your goals to floss daily or master Italian cooking. I mean goals like wanting to be a mentor to someone, wanting to speak at a conference, wanting to learn a new language or technology, etc. Your manager can help suggest goals based on your interests as well as what they've seen others do in your situation. These are goals that help you personally develop into a better engineer, which in turn tends to help your team/company. To me, those are the most important goals.

There are many different frameworks out there for goal setting. For this book, we'll focus on two: SMART and FUN goals. SMART is a great framework for goals whose outcomes are objective, while FUN is the best choice for goals that are subjective and need some flexibility.

SMART

SMART stands for **S**pecific, **M**easurable, **A**ttainable, **R**elevant, and **T**ime-based. For example: *"By the end of March, I will have* *coffee chats with 10 developers at the company."* This framework is incredibly popular with managers because it forces you to write goals that are easy to track and easy to know when they're done. These goals have targets that you can visualize, making it easy to break down the steps to get there. On the downside, not all goals fit the SMART format. And the very clear nature of the end goal makes it very evident when someone has failed to achieve the letter of that goal, even if they have achieved the spirit of it.

FUN

As far as I can tell, FUN goals were developed by Emily Ladau (she's great and you should follow her on Twitter @emily_ladau). FUN stands for:

- **Flexible:** because life happens, things change, and goals shift
- **Uplifting:** because bettering oneself isn't a punishment
- **Numberless:** because your life won't be radically different if you only read 29 books instead of 30.

An example: *"I would like to develop more meaningful relationships with the teams in our org."*

I love this framework for many reasons. First, it centers on goal setting over goal-achieving. To me, the act of thinking about what goals you want to set and how you want to get there is 90% of the value of having goals. Setting aside time to think about what is important to you allows you to focus your effort toward achieving it. And not focusing on measurement or how fast we get there takes a lot of the pressure off.

Second, SMART goals aren't designed to be flexible. They're designed to be objective rather than subjective. While this is helpful when it comes to deciding whether a goal has been completed, it can be really demoralizing to see your goals uncompleted just because something unexpected came up. FUN goals, on the other hand, are flexible by nature. (You could try to make a SMART goal flexible, but that kind of defeats the purpose of them, I think.)

And lastly, the FUN framework puts you, your goals, and your well-being first. It encourages you to grow and to think about what you want for the future, but it doesn't pressure you into getting there.

Once you've figured out what your goals should be — regardless of which framework you use — it's time to start working toward them! Your manager will be helpful here too. You'll meet with them regularly so you can see how you've progressed, talk about any issues or struggles, and receive advice focused on you and your goals.

RECAP
Your manager is a useful tool in helping you accomplish your goals and grow in your career.

Identifying Your Manger's Style
Different managerial styles have their pros and cons. Managers usually work in a combination of styles, so be on the lookout for features of each. Understanding your manager's style will help you work better with them as well as help you understand how to use them effectively.

Identifying and Arranging Opportunities
Your manager can identify opportunities for you to work toward your goals and interests. But the key is that your manager needs to know what you're interested in first. And that means that you have to start thinking about that yourself and talking openly with your manager about it.

Understanding Your Performance

We'd already talked about asking your manager if you're ever unclear about how you're performing, but understanding your performance goes beyond that. There is huge value of walking through your career ladder, understanding the promotions process, and using your manager to get feedback.

Setting and Achieving Goals

Your manager can help you set and achieve goals. SMART is a great framework for goals that are objective in nature, while the FUN framework fits goals that are subjective. Once you've articulated your goals, your manager can help you achieve them by talking about them regularly, helping to unblock you when you're feeling stuck, and offering specific goal-oriented advice.

Bad Managers

J ust as I felt obligated to warn you about bad interviewers after chapter two, I feel the need to talk about bad managers and how to deal with them. What makes for a bad manager? There are varying levels of bad, and there is no one specific thing that makes someone a bad manager, but here are a few things to look out for:

Self-Interest

Your best interests should be very high up on your manager's priority list. It's important that you feel like your manager is pushing you in the direction that you want to go, rather than the direction that works best for them and their self-interest. In fact, self-interest is so damaging in a manager that it's part of the trust equation:

$$\text{Trustworthiness} = \frac{\text{Credibility} + \text{Reliability} + \text{Intimacy}}{\text{Self-Orientation}}$$

The Trust Equation was created by Charles H. Green and has been featured in his books *The Trusted Advisor*, *Trust-Based Selling*, and *The Trusted Advisor Fieldbook*. According to this equation, self-interest is the biggest enemy of trustworthiness. It's okay for your manager to have their own goals and desires. But it's not okay for a manager to steer you in a direction that is not helpful for you simply for their own benefit. It's kind of like a financial planner—you want them to make money, but you want them to be making money because you are making money, not at the expense of your best interests.

Micromanagement

Delegation is a difficult skill to learn, but it's a vital skill for a manager or even a tech lead. While most managers learn to delegate (usually because they have to), not all managers learn that the key to delegation is resisting the urge to micromanage. That is, as long as the person achieves the given goal, it doesn't matter if the person went about it in a different way than how you would have done it. In fact, there might even be a good reason why they decided to do it differently.

Manipulative

Manipulative managers try to force you to do things without your knowledge or consent. They might stoke tensions between engineers, play favorites, or withhold the "good" projects from you if you don't treat them a certain way. On the extreme end of manipulative managers are those who try to blackmail or manage using fear. They'll also retaliate and use the threat of retaliation to manipulate those working for them.

Abusive

These are managers that try to belittle you or who actively work against your self-interests. On the more extreme end, you have managers who abuse power dynamics to make people uncomfortable or even to pray on people sexually. The people most likely to encounter this sort of attitude from a manager are unfortunately non-stereotypical engineers, especially women and trans or non-binary folks. It's important for you to remember that this is never okay. If you see abuse happening to someone else, you have a duty to report it. If it is happening to you, try to stay safe, but get yourself out of that team or company as soon as you can. Nothing is worth taking abuse from people you have to work with daily. We'll talk about this a little bit more in chapter 11.

My hope with this section isn't to scare you off. My hope is to educate you so that you recognize these signs of bad managers so that you can either work to address them or work to get yourself out of those positions. So how do you do that?

ESCAPING A BAD MANAGER

Talk to your Manager? Probably not.

If you fear that you have a bad manager, that manager is probably not the person you want to talk to about it. The only situation in which I would recommend this is if you think that your manager is not doing these things intentionally. But even then, the difficult task of making them aware of that is a lot of pressure to put on yourself. Instead, I would recommend talking to someone else. Anyone that you trust. It could be someone on a different team, a different manager, your skip-level manager, or whomever. If there is no one that you feel comfortable bringing this to, HR is another option. Part of HR's job is to help deal with these kinds of situations.

Transfer teams

If you think it's your manager that's the problem and not the company overall, it's worth considering switching teams. A lot of companies require you to wait for a certain period of time before transferring internally, but if you've been on your current team for a while, you might already be eligible. If a bad manager is your reason for leaving a team, I wouldn't tell them about this until you've already arranged for the transfer.

Leave the Company

You don't owe it to anyone to stick it out in a position where you are being manipulated or abused. If there aren't any opportunities to transfer internally, or if you worry that the same thing will happen on a different team, it might be time to leave the company. There is a lot of stigma around people who leave a job after only a short time, but knowing that, it stands to reason that those people probably left because they had to. If you end up in a situation where someone is asking you about your short tenure at one or more jobs, especially if it's due to negative experiences, I recommend saying something like *"I had some bad experiences there and realized that it wasn't a good environment for me. I'd prefer not to go into more detail about it."* A good interviewer will hopefully be able to take the hint and move around it gracefully.

CHAPTER SEVEN

Feedback, Anyone?

*"Continuous delivery without continuous
feedback is very, very dangerous."*

— Colin Humphreys

F eedback is a gift. But it's a gift that we often look upon like a pair of socks or a Christmas sweater — something decent at best or wildly unflattering at worst. But there is a reason for that: most people suck at feedback. They suck at asking for it, they suck at receiving it, and they suck at delivering it. Knowing that, it's no wonder people dread giving and receiving feedback!

Luckily, these are skills that we can learn like any other. As with some of the previous topics, there has been a lot written about feedback. My goal here is to distill some of that into manageable takeaways and add in my two cents where appropriate. For anyone interested in drilling down further into giving and receiving feedback, I'll include some resources in the appendix.

ASKING FOR FEEDBACK

*"To avoid criticism, do nothing,
say nothing, and be nothing."*

– Elbert Hubbard

Not a lot of people actually *ask* for feedback. And when they do, they tend not to get the kind of feedback that they're looking for. To understand why, it's important to look at the different types of feedback. In their book *Thanks for the Feedback,* Douglas Stone and Sheila Heen talk about how feedback can be categorized into three major types:

- **Appreciation:** The recognition of work that has already happened or is ongoing. This type of feedback motivates and connects people and is vital for high performance.
- **Coaching:** Feedback that is intended to help a person grow, usually delivered over a period of time while the person is trying to achieve a goal.

- **Evaluation:** An assessment against a set of standards. Most notably, a performance review.

A problem can occur when the person asking for feedback expects one type and the person receiving it gives another. For example:

Let's say that I ask my manager for feedback, because I'm looking for coaching on the new project that I'm working on. My manager tells me that I'm right on track to deliver my project on schedule, and that if I do, my promotion is in the bag. In this situation, I asked for feedback and my manager gave it to me. However, I'm walking away feeling like I didn't get the coaching feedback that I needed, and my manager is walking away feeling like they did a great job of giving me impromptu appreciating feedback.

That's what Stone and Heen call a "feedback mismatch."

Ask for Specific Feedback

The best way to avoid this situation is to be clear about what kind of feedback you're looking for. When asking for feedback from others, people will often ask some variation of *"How am I doing?"* In my opinion, that's too broad of a question, especially if you're looking for feedback on something specific. To get the targeted feedback you're looking for, try coming up with specific questions ahead of time. For instance:

- *"Am I on track to get promoted in January?"* (Evaluation)
- *"I'm worried that I'm not making enough progress on my project. I feel like I'm stuck on X. How would you handle it?"* (Coaching)
- *"Can you help me structure milestones on my project?"* (Coaching)

Specific questions like these are much more likely to get you the response you need. Asking for feedback can sometimes feel a lot like asking for help, which is why people tend to shy away from it. But actually, it's the people who ask for help that grow the fastest. In fact, it shows great self-awareness and maturity to ask for feedback, especially when things aren't going well.

Feedback is Awkward. Ask Anyways.

People often don't think that they can ask for feedback directly from their peers. They look to their manager to gather feedback for them. In all honesty, giving and receiving regular feedback with your peers will not only ensure that you have the information that you need to grow, but it will also help your team collaborate better.

A team that gives each other feedback on a regular basis is a team that is thinking critically about what they're working on. They're more likely to ask questions and give constructive criticism in the moment, and those things are more likely to be taken well by others. In short, if we stop pretending like we're perfect and we know everything (or hiding because we're scared we know nothing), we're significantly more productive.

Give Feedback to Get Feedback

The best way to get feedback is to offer feedback to others. Giving regular, constructive feedback at appropriate moments gives people the sense that you care about their growth. In my experience, the more feedback you're giving people on a regular basis, the more feedback you'll receive in turn. And the quality of the feedback you receive will also be determined by the quality of the feedback that you give.

RECEIVING FEEDBACK

Some people fear feedback because certain types of feedback can be hard to receive. Let's start with figuring out how you like to receive feedback in general.

How Do You Like to Receive Feedback?

Everyone is a little bit different in how they best handle and process feedback. Some people like to hear about it right in the moment so that they don't waste any time; others like to wait until specific points, like 1:1s or performance reviews. Some people prefer to receive feedback in writing ahead of time so that they can process it before discussing, while others want to be able to ask questions right away. Some people like feedback to be as direct as possible; others prefer a more indirect approach. I would also think about what type(s) of feedback (from the three types above) you're usually most interested in. Knowing exactly how you like to receive your feedback will make it easier for others to give you that feedback in the best way possible for you to process it.

Sitting with Difficult Feedback

Anyone who has ever taken a risk or tried to learn something new has been told at some point that they've done something wrong or that they have areas in which they need to improve. Hearing this can really sting. Though it's just a sign of growth, and hopefully you've never expected yourself to be absolutely perfect at everything, that knowledge does little to help ease the hurt.

Now, if you're anything like me, negative feedback (even when it's meant to be constructive) is going to make you feel like you're backed into a corner. Especially if it's something that surprises you. And when I'm backed into a corner, I have a tendency to get defensive. It becomes really important to me that the other person understand the intention of my actions, or the context of the situation. This is an adrenaline response, also known as a fight, flight, or freeze (F/F/F) response.

Responses like this happen most often when the feedback is something that is incongruent with your self-identity. For example, my identity is based heavily on being a good manager to the people on my teams. Is that healthy? Yes and no. But that's a point for another book. And so, if someone gives me feedback like "some people on your team don't feel very comfortable talking to you," then it feels like my identity is being attacked. Hence the lashing out. But that doesn't get me anywhere. First, if the feedback is true, then I'm missing out on an area for me to grow. And second, it doesn't leave a good impression for the person giving me feedback. They might feel less inclined to do so in the future as a result.

So how do we prevent this from happening? By taking the time to let your F/F/F response subside and process difficult feedback before responding to it.

Personally, I like to receive feedback in writing *before* talking about it for this reason. It allows me to get over the initial shock, think critically about the feedback, and then have a productive discussion. But you won't always be made aware of the feedback ahead of time, so it's important to learn how to sit with difficult feedback in the moment.

First, take a deep breath. Count to ten, close your eyes, do whatever works for you normally to calm yourself down. Let the words sink in. Once you no longer feel like your heart is racing, then you're ready to start processing the feedback rationally. It's okay to be quiet for a bit, or even to say that you need some time (whether it's a few minutes or a few days) to process. People often assume that they need to respond right away, but that's usually the worst option. If you respond right away, you're going with an F/F/F response — most likely fight. Instead, taking a moment or asking for time shows that you've listened to what your teammate has to say and that you care enough to carefully reflect on it. If you feel you can't calm yourself down in the moment and need to get yourself out of the situation, this is also a good strategy.

The next step is to think about where the person's feedback differs from your understanding of the situation. We often do this automatically, but with the wrong intent: We look for where the other person is wrong. Because if their feedback is wrong, then we don't have to feel bad about our own actions. But instead of looking for wrongness, we're going to focus on the difference. Telling someone that they are wrong shuts down the conversation. Noticing a difference between how you understand things and how the other person understands things allows you to ask questions.

For example, maybe you thought that you were finishing all of your projects on time. But in a 1:1 with your manager, she tells you that she has noticed you taking longer than she would expect to complete your projects. Your immediate thought would probably be *"But I've been completing all of my tasks on time!"* That's your brain looking for wrongness. It would come off as defensive if you said that. But your brain has identified an area of difference between your understanding and your manager's. So it's important to try to resolve that difference. Try saying instead something like:

- *"I thought that I've been completing my projects as scheduled. Is my understanding wrong?"*
- *"What makes you think that?"*
- *"What would you normally expect?"*
- *"How so?"*

Notice something about these suggestions: all of them end with a question mark, not an exclamation point. If you're making statements (or exclamations), you're likely trying to disprove the feedback. If you're asking questions, you're trying to understand the feedback. You're keeping the conversation going instead of shutting it down. Not only that, you might actually get some clarification.

In our example situation, if you ask instead *"How so?"* your manager might tell you something like *"I know you've been completing your projects on time, I just worry that you're estimating that those projects will take more time than I would expect."* By asking that simple question, you learn that the issue is not whether you're delivering things on time, it's whether the deadlines that you're setting for yourself are too padded. Asking questions like this will help you get to the root of the problem so you can better address it.

Following Up on Feedback

Something that I think gets overlooked in the feedback process is following up on the feedback you receive. Especially if you're given feedback on an opportunity area, it's a great idea to go back to that person and ask how things are going once you've taken steps toward addressing it. Not only does this help you in terms of knowing whether you've addressed the opportunity area, but it shows the person that you took their feedback to heart.

DELIVERING FEEDBACK

Receiving feedback is hard, but delivering feedback — and doing so effectively — can be difficult too. If you go about giving feedback the wrong way, the person will likely shut down and you will have accomplished nothing except to make them angry. Like I said earlier, I'll defer most of the details on delivering feedback to people smarter than me (see again Stone and Heen's brilliant book *Thanks for the Feedback*). *But I do want to cover a few specific points.*

How Does the Person Like to Receive Feedback?

Just like it was important for you to know how you like to receive feedback to mitigate your F/F/F response, it's important to know how others like to receive feedback to avoid setting off theirs. I've seen a fair number of issues come up between people when it comes to feedback, usually when personalities and cultural differences clash. For instance, someone who is normally very direct might come across as confrontational to someone who is less direct.

Why should you care? Well, if your intent in giving the feedback is to help the other person, your feedback is going to go a lot farther if you deliver it in a way that's most palatable for them.

The best way to find out how a person likes to receive feedback is simply to ask them. It's usually one of the things I ask when first meeting someone whom I'm going to be working closely with.

That way, when I have feedback for that person, I know the best way to deliver it.

Why Is Radical Candor Almost Always Best?

Speaking of, let's talk about the actual delivery. In Kim Scott's book *Radical Candor*, she talks about a framework that divides feedback into four quadrants: Manipulative Insincerity, Ruinous Empathy, Obnoxious Aggression, and Radical Candor.

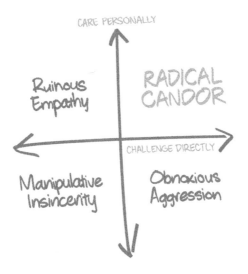

I'll let her tackle the first three and we can just look at the last one. Radical candor is the intersection of caring personally and challenging directly. When we care personally, we are showing the other person that we're putting their needs before our own. And when we challenge directly, we give people the kind of heads up that underlies human decency.

Radical candor allows us to show that we care personally about the other person and their growth by challenging them directly, instead of avoiding giving any constructive feedback or giving feedback in less constructive ways. This doesn't mean that you have to be rude about the feedback, just direct.

RECAP

Giving feedback, receiving feedback, asking for feedback — none of it is easy. But honest feedback is incredibly important both for helping others and for accepting help from others. Here's what we covered:

Asking for Feedback

There are three different types of feedback: appreciation, coaching, and evaluation. If you receive a different type of feedback than you were expecting, that mismatch might make you feel like you didn't get the support you were looking for while the other person feels like they've done a great job. So it's best to ask for specific feedback, and you can go about it is directly, through your manager, and by offering others regular feedback to invite that sort of communication within the team.

Receiving Feedback

How do you personally like to receive feedback? Make sure that the people around you know, so that they feel comfortable giving it to you. Once you've gotten people to give you feedback, you need to be able to handle difficult feedback. De-escalate your body's natural response and then ask questions. And once you've addressed the feedback, follow up with the person who gave it to you. This builds trust and increases the likelihood that they'll give you feedback in the future.

Delivering Feedback

Understanding how other people like to receive feedback is just as important as learning how you prefer it yourself. By knowing this, you're less likely to trigger their F/F/F response and more likely to have a constructive interaction. And unless you know specifically that the person doesn't respond well to it, deliver feedback with radical candor — it's a great framework for showing that you not

only care personally but that you want to see them grow and are
willing to push them toward it.

If you'd like to learn more about giving and receiving feedback —
and I highly suggest that you do — I would recommend reading
the two books that I mentioned in this chapter, *Thanks for the
Feedback* by Douglas Stone and Sheila Heen and *Radical Candor*
by Kim Scott.

PART THREE

NAVIGATING YOUR CAREER

CHAPTER EIGHT

Establishing a Study Group

"To acquire knowledge, one must study;
but to acquire wisdom, one must observe."

— Marilyn vos Savant

One of the best ways to make real progress as quickly as possible is by establishing a study group. If you've just graduated from college or a coding bootcamp, you might have thought that was the end of studying and study groups. Not so fast! A work study group is very similar to a class study group, and you can benefit in the same ways by being a part of one. It's a group of people who are in roughly the same place in their career who are looking to achieve similar goals. But instead of studying for a test, you're studying to achieve your goals.

THE BENEFITS OF A STUDY GROUP
Study groups have three main benefits:

Learning From the Successes and Mistakes of Others
Everybody makes mistakes. They suck, you learn from them, and then you move on. But what if you got to learn from more than just your own mistakes? You can actually learn a lot from the experiences of others, whether they're successes or mistakes. In a study group, you suddenly have access to everyone else's recent experiences, and you have the chance to ask questions and see what you can learn from them.

Comparing Notes
Maybe your manager said or did something that you found strange. Do other junior developers have to get coffee for their managers? Or maybe you're wondering how other junior developers got comfortable with the codebase so quickly. It can feel awkward asking people questions like these. Especially people who are on more senior and/or on your team. The nice thing about having a group of peers you can compare notes with is that you have people you can go to with questions like this without fear of judgement.

Support System
You hopefully have people in your life who you can turn to for support. But sometimes it's nice to have someone who works at the same company and knows exactly what you're talking about.

HOW DO I ESTABLISH ONE?

Just like when you were building your network, there are a few different ways to find people in order to establish a study group. If you're at a larger company, it's very likely that you'll have other people who started on the same day or within the same few weeks as you. If you connected with any of them in your new hire orientation or during your first few weeks, they could be good people to approach.

If you're looking to start a study group later on, think about the people that you interact with on a regular basis. They could be on the same team as you, or they could be on different teams. Look for people who are in similar situations as you and who have similar goals.

If you're still having trouble finding people, I would suggest talking to your manager and your mentor about it. They might know some people who are in similar positions, or they can ask around to see if any other managers know of someone.

WHAT SHOULD A STUDY GROUP DO?

So now that you've formed your study group, what should you actually do?

Meet Regularly

This might go without saying, but I highly recommend setting up a recurring time for you all to meet. If you try organizing meetings "as needed," you'll find that you meet less frequently than you do if you have a regularly scheduled meetup. That's because people tend to think that they don't have much to talk about. But you'll find that if you create the time and space, you actually have a lot more that you want to talk and learn about than you think.

In addition to this, I would recommend setting up some sort of regular communication channel, like a private channel on Slack, Microsoft Teams, or even a text chain. It never hurts to develop additional rapport, and you never know when you'll need someone to turn to.

Talk About What Has Gone Well

Now that you're getting together on a regular basis, the next thing you should do is figure out what to talk about. And what could be better than talking about the things that are going well? It's amazing what you can learn from other's successes. As you're listening to others recount their experiences, ask yourself: How would you have handled that situation? What can you learn from it?

Talk About What Hasn't Gone Well

It can be hard to talk about the things that haven't gone well. Hopefully you've been able to establish a certain level of psychological safety with your study group, because that will make it a lot easier to share the things that have gone wrong. By sharing these experiences too, you not only help the others in the group to avoid similar mistakes, but you also reinforce the lessons that you learned.

The best way to draw lessons from your mistakes and reflect on your learning is to ask questions. One interesting question is whether the bad thing would have happened if you were on another team. This is a way of understanding whether the thing that went wrong was specific to your team and situation or if it was something to be cautious about in general. Making mistakes never feels good, but they're a normal part of growth. Whatever the mistake, it's important to learn from it.

Book Club

Starting a book club with your study group can boost all of your learning and make absorbing the material more fun. You could read books about software engineering, career development, giving feedback, or even leadership. Check out the appendix for some recommendations. Having a group of people reading and discussing the same book helps the material sink in deeper. Plus, you're more likely to stay accountable in a group. And you don't have to limit yourself to just books. Maybe there is an online course available on a new technology or framework. Or maybe you each decide to attend a different tech conference and then share notes with each other. Yes, books are the traditional medium for new learning, but the sky and your imagination are really the only limits.

RECAP

Now that you've got your study group set up, you're really ready to accomplish your goals in record time! Here's what we covered in this chapter:

Benefits of a Study Group

Study groups are great! They're groups of likeminded individuals who have similar goals. These groups of people, roughly at the same point in their careers, share their experiences in an effort to learn from each others' successes and mistakes; it can grow your learning exponentially. Study groups can also be useful as safe spaces to talk about things that are too awkward to discuss with your manager or team, like *"Does every team have hour-long standups?"* Having a study group also means that you have an at-work support system that knows about things at the company, so you don't have to explain everything to them.

How Do I Establish One?

Establishing a study group sounds hard, but it doesn't have to be. For those who are just starting out at a company, the group of people who started around the same time as you isa great place to start. You might also think about forming a study group with the people that you work with, whether on your own team or another. And if all else fails, asking your manager or mentor can be a really helpful because they'll either know people or they'll be able to ask around and help you find people.

What Should a Study Group Do?

Set up regular meetings, because even though you might not think you have anything to talk about, things will always emerge if you create space to talk about them. Asking questions like *"What has gone well?"* and *"What hasn't gone well?"* is a good place to start.

A book club is another great idea of something to do with your group, whether its books on software engineering, books on career development (like this one!), or anything else that you think would be helpful.

CHAPTER NINE

Career Paths & Levels

O nce you've settled into your new job and are starting to feel comfortable, it's a good time to start thinking about your future. What is it you'd like to be doing in the next six months? One year? Three years? Even 20 years!

It's hard to start answering these questions without having an idea of what different career paths look like. And while these paths might vary a little bit from company to company, my hope is that the descriptions that I provide below are generic enough to give you an idea of the scope and responsibilities of each of these roles and paths.

I bring this up because as a manager, I frequently see a mis-understanding about what it means to go beyond senior engineer. People often think that being a staff engineer means that you're doing all of the things that you were doing as a senior engineer, just… *better.* But in reality, it's a lot more complicated than that. A staff engineer's role is significantly different than that of a senior engineer, as we'll discover below. My suggestion is that you read about these roles and really understand what is expected in each before you try going after them. I know people both on the engineering and managerial tracks who have regretted getting promoted because the job becomes a fundamentally different one at the next level. That's not to say that you shouldn't go after these roles if it's what you want, but just make sure that you know what you're getting into.

But first, let's look at why titles matter.

WHY TITLES MATTER (AND WHY THEY SHOULDN'T)

Titles shouldn't matter, but they do. All too often, titles create a pseudo-hierarchy that shouldn't actually exist. Why do titles suck? Many reasons:

1. Titles make junior developers afraid to speak up and offer ideas that are different or contrary to senior developers.

2. Titles encourage the idea that there is a gap between junior and mid-level engineers, and between mid-level and senior ones. Often, a high-performing mid-level engineer is actually performing at the same level as a senior engineer, only without the title.

3. Titles give the false impression that knowledge is hierarchical. That is, they lead us to believe that mid-level engineers know everything a junior engineer knows, *plus* some extra.

But at the same time, job titles are important when it comes to getting your next job. If you spent 5-10 years working at one company as a "Software Engineer," it's going to be harder for you to get a job as a senior engineer than if you had a "Senior Software Engineer" title. And as hard as it might be for someone traditionally represented in tech to be given that title, it's going to be at least ten times harder for others.

Not to mention, at a vast majority of companies, pay is directly correlated with job title. Companies with specific job titles often have pay bands associated with each title. The idea being that as you progress from junior to mid-level to senior, you progress through the pay bands and they help ensure that you're being paid fairly compared to your peers. But at a company without titles, it creates a whole lot of ambiguity that makes it really easy to hide pay inequities, whether they're conscious or not. If two people with the title "Developer" are making $100k and $500k respectively, it's really hard to know if the developer making $100k is being paid fairly compared to their peers. Is the other "Developer" at a level where they deserve to be earning $500k? Or are both of these developers at the same relative level and the first is being underpaid? Who knows?

And as with many injustices within tech, the issues around titles disproportionately affect underrepresented minorities in tech. This is because the tech industry is rampant with sexism, racism, ableism, ageism, etc. You name it, I've seen it. Sometimes it's obvious, but a lot of the time it's more subtle. An engineer who is a black woman, for example, might not initially get the respect that she deserves in a meeting with a group of people who don't know her. I've heard countless stories of people assuming that women in meetings are product managers, designers, QA, etc. And even when faced with the fact that she is an engineer, they'll assume she's more junior than she is. All of this means that this engineer is much less likely to be heard or taken seriously than another engineer who more closely fits the stereotype. It's disgusting but it does happen and should be called out whenever you see it.

So long story short: there are a lot of problems with job titles and the barriers that they can create. But not caring about job titles is a privilege in a world where a lot of people must really go the extra mile to dot their I's and cross their T's to even be taken seriously.

Now that we've talked about *why* titles are important, let's talk about some of these titles.

APPRENTICE ENGINEER

Only a subset of companies have programs like this, but I feel like it's especially important to talk about them because they do an amazing job of providing a foot in the door for people who might need a bridge between a coding bootcamp (or being self-taught) and working full time as an entry-level engineer. These programs vary wildly but are an amazing resource both to the companies who offer them and to the engineers that participate in them. I've seen some truly amazing engineers come out of these programs.

At Twitter, for instance, at the time of writing this, we have an Apprenticeship program where we hire the types of people mentioned above who need that bridge and have them go through what is essentially a year-long internship. During this program, apprentices work with one or two different teams and get to work on real-world projects. The goal is that with the support of their mentor, their teams, the other apprentices, and the program in general, these fledgling engineers will be able to grow into entry-level engineers by the end of that first year.

As an apprentice or similar, your role is mainly to learn as much as you can. You'll be learning about the tech stack that the team uses, how to work with a team, and how code gets written, tested, and deployed. The expectation is that your mentor will spend a lot of time with you at first and then ease off as you become more comfortable and independent.

I highly recommend programs like this if you are looking to get your foot in the door. You learn a ton, you meet a lot of people, you get paid, and hopefully it leads into a full-time engineer position!

If you participated in a coding boot camp, I would suggest asking them about these programs. Boot camps will often partner with companies to feed into programs like these, so they would be a good place to start.

ENTRY-LEVEL ENGINEER

Different companies have different names for engineers at this level. Expect titles like "Software Engineer," "Junior Software Engineer," "Associate Software Engineer," "Software Engineer I," etc. Engineers at this level will likely be a year or two out of college, or will have a year or two of professional work experience. I like to describe these roles using a combination of lenses:

First is scope, which is the area that you're expected to occupy. For instance, as an entry-level engineer, I expect their scope to be themselves. They take on work, they focus on their own work, and aren't expected to think about the bigger picture yet — though many do.

Second is independence, which is how much support you need in order to get your work done. As an entry-level engineer, I expect a person to lean on me (their manager), their tech lead, and/or their mentor heavily. We'll probably be their go-to for all questions, and we'll direct them to the right person who can give them answers. This is often because entry-level engineers don't yet understand who is responsible for what and haven't developed the relationships that they need in order to know who to ask.

And lastly is complexity, which looks at how much ambiguity the engineer can handle. Entry-level engineers aren't expected to handle much ambiguity. The expectation is that they will receive tasks and projects that have been clearly defined, over a small problem set, and that can be completed in a few days to a few weeks.

As entry-level engineers become more comfortable, gradually they start working more like mid-level engineers, which we'll look at next.

MID-LEVEL ENGINEER

Again, you'll see many different names here: "Software Engineer II," "Software Engineer," "Mid-Level Engineer," etc. Engineers at this level will have at least a few years of experience. If we look at the mid-level role using our three lenses, we can define it as:

Scope: The scope of a mid-level engineer is themselves *plus* the people around them. Note that this doesn't necessarily mean the whole team. This might mean that they are working closely with a junior engineer, or they're partnered up with another engineer on a project. While a junior engineer might not have a ton of context as to what's going on beyond their work, a mid-level engineer will have a general idea of how their work fits into what the rest of the team is working on.

Independence: *Somewhat* independent. I still expect mid-level engineers to be asking questions, but now I expect that a majority of those questions will be asked directly to the people who have the answers instead of me having to direct them to the right person. I also expect engineers at this level to be able to take on slightly larger projects than they could as junior engineers. And finally, I expect mid-level engineers to be able to unblock themselves in simple situations, rather than needing someone to jump in.

Complexity: Projects at this level might have some ambiguity. The questions that need to be answered usually aren't large architectural or design decisions where we're starting from scratch. Usually, the problem and the expected outcome will be clear, but there will be a variety of ways the outcome could be achieved. An engineer at this level could be reasonably expected to break down a medium to large project into smaller chunks that could be taken on by themselves or a junior engineer.

SENIOR ENGINEER

There is more title standardization at this level; most engineers at this level are simply called "Senior Engineer." Engineers at this level will generally have at least three to five years of experience. If we look at senior engineers using our three lenses, we can define the role as:

Scope: The scope of a senior engineer is their team. This means that they have a lot of context and insight into the work that the team is doing as a whole. They're probably working with other senior engineers, as well as junior and mid-level ones. Senior engineers are seen as a subject matter expert in at least one or two areas and people come to them with related questions.

Independence: *Fairly* independent. Sometimes I describe this as *fully* independent, but I think that's a bit misleading, because everyone at every level needs some support. But what I mean here is that I expect to get fewer questions from a senior engineer, and that those questions will be less about how to implement and more around the details of a project, expected outcomes, "have we thought about X," etc. If a senior engineer comes to a roadblock, I can reasonably expect them to unblock themselves, or to use me or their PM to help unblock them.

Complexity: Senior engineers should expect ambiguity. Projects at this level are usually ones that don't have simple, straightforward solutions because they're often breaking new ground. The problem or the result might not be clear. There will have large architectural or design decisions that the senior engineer will need to make. An engineer at this level could be reasonably expected to break down a large, complex project into smaller chunks that could be taken on by themselves or other engineers. In the case of these larger projects, they're often the ones driving the work and supporting the other engineers working on the project.

TERMINAL ROLES

Before we start looking at what can happen beyond senior engineer, I think it's important to talk about what we call "terminal roles." These are roles/levels at which we consider it acceptable to stay indefinitely. Senior engineer is often one of these roles. A person can become a senior engineer and stay there for their entire career if that's what makes them happy. In fact, I know a lot of senior engineers who do just that.

But if you choose to go beyond the level of senior engineer, here is where our path begins to split into two at a lot of companies. I'll talk about each path below, but I want to make it clear that these are not paths that are set in stone. In fact, it's better to think of it less of a career ladder (which implies that you can only move up or down) and more of a career jungle gym (wherein you can move up, down, sideways, and slantways). A lot of people spend their careers jumping back and forth between these two paths. Some people even swear by what they call the Engineering/Management Pendulum, which postulates that it's best for managers to have relatively recent development experience, so you should jump back and forth between management and hands-on development to keep your skills fresh. I say do whatever makes you happy!

ENGINEERING PATH: STAFF ENGINEER AND BEYOND

Most people think that in order to continue moving up at a company, you eventually *have* to become a manager. This can be the case at some companies where there isn't a career ladder for individual contributors (ICs) beyond senior or staff level. But some companies have IC roles that go all the way up to VP or even Senior VP levels! Let's look at some of these roles and what they entail.

Staff Engineer

Some companies might have a "Senior Engineer II" role, or some might jump straight to calling it "Principal Engineer." But more often than not, they call it "Staff Engineer." Like I said above, the role of a staff engineer is fundamentally different than that of a senior engineer. Let's look at it through our lenses:

Scope: The scope of a senior engineer is their team. For a staff engineer, we add nearby teams to their scope. This could mean working on projects, architectures, or processes for their own team and then driving the adoption of similar work on other teams who might also benefit. It could also mean leading projects that require a multi-team effort, things like driving the adoption of better automated testing or the adoption of a new technology.

Independence: *Fairly* independent. I'm going to use the same word here. You can argue that a staff engineer is slightly more independent than a senior engineer, if only because they're actively building their own relationships with other teams so that they're able to know how best they can help. They use these relationships to help influence decision-making. Depending on the company and the organization, a staff engineer might report to the manager of their team or to the organization's director.

Complexity: Very ambiguous. The projects that staff engineers work on are often the result of them noticing a gap and convincing others that it needs to be addressed. The timelines of their projects can stretch into many months and often don't have clear stopping points. As such, staff engineers need to be able to answer questions like:

1. *"How broadly will this work benefit other teams?"*
2. *"What is an appropriate stopping point? At what point are we getting diminishing returns?"*
3. *"What is the impact of this work to the company?"*
4. *"How does this work align with where we want our codebase to be in two years?"*

As you can see, a staff engineer isn't just a "really good senior engineer." They play a different role altogether. This is also why I tell people that being a tech lead is a bad steppingstone if they want to become a staff engineer. As a tech lead, it's hard to be thinking about the teams around you when you're focused on the inner workings of your own team. Both senior and staff engineers play important roles, and you should only try to get promoted to staff if that's the role that you want to play.

Senior Staff Engineer and Beyond

Beyond the staff engineer level, the levels become less clear cut. You start to see titles like "Senior Staff Engineer," "Principal Engineer," "Distinguished Engineer," "Engineering Fellow," etc. Not all companies have purely individual contributor roles at these levels, so if you're looking to go down this path, it's worth finding out how far your company's engineering track goes.

I'm not going to talk a whole lot about what these levels are like, because each role at a particular company tends to be pretty unique. As you keep going down the engineering path, your scope increases to larger and larger parts of the company, and the work that you take on is more and more ambiguous. Because of this, the path from one level to the next is also unique. While the path from a junior to mid-level — or even a mid-level to senior — is pretty straight-forward, the path at these higher levels really depends on the company, the organization, and their particular needs. You'll have to work with your manager to help identify what it is that you would like to do as an individual contributor engineer and what the path looks like to get there.

MANAGEMENT PATH: ENGINEERING MANAGER AND BEYOND

This path focuses on the development and support of engineers to unlock their full potential. In an effort to not re-invent the wheel, I'm going to give a brief overview of some of these roles. If you would like to learn more, I highly recommend Camille Fournier's book *The Manager's Path*.

Engineering Manager

This is the first stop on the management path. As an engineering manager, you'll likely be managing a small-to-medium sized team of people — between three and eight engineers. When you first start out, it'll probably be on the lower end, with more members added as you get more comfortable and your team grows. Just like with the technical path, we can describe these management roles via a few lenses:

Scope of Accountability: The scope of an engineering manager is their own team. They're actively involved with the team's day-to-day and sprint-to-sprint efforts, as well as quarterly planning.

Responsibility: Given a clear objective, an engineering manager is expected to come up with concrete action items to achieve that objective. Their manager or director will hold them accountable to those action.

Senior Engineering Manager

Congratulations! You've been promoted. You likely grew your team, both in size and in scope. And you have proven your ability to influence others throughout your organization. Like the jump between a senior and staff engineer, though, there is a similar jump between manager and senior manager. Let's look at what is different:

Scope of Accountability: You probably overlook one large team or a few smaller teams that report up to you.

Responsibility: Given a strategy, a senior engineering manager is expected to come up with a set of clear objectives that will lead to achieving that strategy.

Being a senior manager often feels different than being an engineering manager. You're no longer focusing on individual projects; you've abstracted that layer. You're likely not dealing with ICs daily anymore, and are dealing with tech leads and managers instead. Some people like the idea of working at this level and some people don't. Personally, I think the idea of growing leaders and managers is incredibly satisfying and fulfilling, so I'm okay with that layer of abstraction. But being an engineering manager is also usually considered a terminal role, so you don't have to move up to senior management if you don't want to. As always, it's important to learn more about what the next level entails and make an informed decision.

Associate Director, Director, and Beyond

As you continue to move up the ladder, your scope of accountability continues to increase. You'll start managing entire organizations or groups of organizations. Your responsibilities change as well. You might be given a mission and asked to come up with strategies for achieving that mission. You might even be asked to come up with what the company's mission should be in the first place! The higher up you go, the further out you're looking on the time horizon and the more you've abstracted the work going on below you.

I don't have any experience at these levels yet, so like I mentioned earlier, I highly recommend checking out *The Manager's Path* and learning from someone who has actually lived it firsthand.

The Trap of Being a Manager-Doer

It goes by many names — manager-doer and hands-on manager are two examples— but it's almost always a trap. People get sucked in by the idea of being able to have their cake and eat it too. They like management, but they still want to stay technical and write code. But it's a really difficult place to be. If you have a small team (no more than 2-4 engineers), you *might* be able to get away with straddling these two roles. But any larger or more complex and one of three things will happen:

1. You'll spend too much time on the development side of things and fall behind on your management tasks. You'll lose focus of the bigger picture and your team's planning will suffer as a result. You won't be able to spend as much time supporting the people on your team and they might resent you for that.

2. You'll take on engineering tasks but get caught up with the work of managing a team. The engineering tasks will take a long time for you to complete, if you're able to complete them at all. Other projects that depend on the work you're doing will be blocked as a result and you'll make everyone's life more difficult. Your team will also resent you for that.

3. You'll try to give both sides of things 100% of your time and energy. The only way to do this is to work overtime. You'll quickly start to burn out, forget things, and look for shortcuts. You'll resent yourself for it.

I definitely pushed all three examples to their extremes, but for the purpose of showing that none of these three paths ends with you or your team being happy. And even if the results aren't quite as extreme as I've described above, they will still be similar and real.

As an individual contributor, you're focusing on the impact of your own work. As a manager, you're focusing on the impact of your *team's* work. Trying to combine the two almost always ends badly because they're so different. It's like trying to see the forest *and* the trees. This is why the idea of a "hands-on manager" or "manager-doer" is a big red flag to me.

RECAP

Eight chapters down, three more to go! In this chapter, we looked at career paths and titles For the purpose of this recap, I've included all of the titles below staff engineer in "The Technical Path".

Why Titles Matter (and Why They Shouldn't)

Titles are important when it comes to ensuring that people are paid fairly. They are also helpful when it comes to switching jobs, because it gives other companies a snapshot of your abilities. But titles can also be used to belittle, discourage junior engineers from speaking up, and to confer status where it may or may not be warranted.

The Technical Path

Nowadays, companies often have robust paths for people who want to stay technical and hands-on. You can go from being an apprentice or junior developer, where your responsibilities are mostly doing your own work, to a principal engineer or beyond, where you're responsible for large pieces of a company's codebase, if not the entirety of it. Once you get to senior engineer, however, it's important to pause and think about whether you want to continue forward to the levels beyond, where the job becomes fairly different from that of an individual contributor engineer. It's perfectly okay to stay at a senior level if that's what makes you happy.

The Management Path

And then there's the managerial side of things. It's important to think about what kind of scope and level of abstraction you're looking for. If you're looking to be right where the action is, a manager role is best for you. If you like to think more big picture, maybe you'll like being a senior manager or beyond. Just whatever you do, avoid pitfalls of being a "manager-doer." For a more in-depth look at what it is to be a manager, I highly recommend reading *The Manager's Path* by Camille Fournier.

CHAPTER TEN

Getting Promoted

"People don't get promoted for doing their jobs really well. They get promoted by demonstrating their potential to do more."

— Tara Jaye Frank

I f you're starting to think about a promotion, congratulations! You're probably made the most out of your first 90 days and really set yourself up for success in the next 90. You might have used your manager effectively, worked hard to address people's feedback, and maybe even set up a study group to focus on growth and learning. In short, it sounds like you're in a really good place. And I think it's good to take a moment to celebrate that.

Now that we're here, let's figure out how to get promoted. Note that I talk about how to "get promoted," and not necessarily things like "deserving" or "asking" for a promotion. Like I've said several times throughout this book, your career is in your own hands. Whether or not you have a manager or a mentor who is looking out for you and actively helping you grow, it's important for you to be the driver.

UNDERSTANDING THE PROMOTIONS PROCESS

Your chances of getting promoted are much better if you understand the promotions process. That includes knowing the answer to a few key questions. If you've been following along with the book, it's likely you've already talked to your manager about some or all of this.

Who Makes the Decisions?

A lot of decisions get made by many different people during the promotions process. Who decides whether you're ready to be put up for a promotion? Most likely this will be your direct manager. After that, who decides whether your promotion succeeds or fails? Is it a single person? Is it a committee?

It's important to know these things because you're going to have to view things from the perspective of those making these decisions. If the decisionmaker is someone who already has context about you, like your skip-level manager, then it's probably going to be easier for them to understand your impact and support your promotion. But if it is someone in a completely different part of the organization, you'll likely have to put in more effort to explain your projects and their impact to get yourself promoted.

How Often are Promotions Processed?

Some companies process promotions only once or twice a year, usually at the same time that they do performance reviews. Other companies process promotions quarterly or even monthly. The less frequently these things happen, the more certain you'll want to be at the point when your manager puts you up for promotion. After all, if the next time you can get put up for a promotion is a year from now, the stakes are much higher than if it could happen again next month.

What Information is Needed to Justify the Promotion?

This is a big one. If you've talked to your manager about career paths and the promotions process, you probably have a good idea of what it means to be performing at the next level. But that can be different than what it takes to convince someone else that you're operating at the next level. Whoever is deciding on your promotion will probably be looking at your "impact." But as we'll see about below, impact is often hard to define. So how do you make sure that you're demonstrating it? Find out what other people have done to get promoted to the level you're aiming for. The more recent the promotion, the better. Your manager should be able to help you out with this. By looking at the impact a few different people showed to justify their promotions, it gets easier to get a feel for where the bar is set.

DEMONSTRATING IMPACT

So how do you actually demonstrate that fuzzy concept of impact? It all starts at the beginning of your project. At the start of each project, I would recommend thinking about what sort of impact the project will have on your stakeholders, whether that's other teams within your company, customers, users, whomever. How can you best demonstrate that impact? With cold hard data! If you're working on a project related to the checkout page of an eCommerce site, you might measure impact based on conversion rate, average order size, or number of add-ons sold. If you're working on a media player for a social media company, you might look at how long people are watching videos or how many videos the average user watches. And if you're working on ads, you can think about how your project has affected advertiser spend. If you're having trouble figuring out how to measure this impact, talk to your manager or product manager about it. Next, you want to make sure you actually gather the data that you hope will show your impact. Often, we're talking about metrics that are already being gathered, like daily active users, conversion rate, or click-through rate. If that's the case, then it's easy! Just make sure you grab the data at the end of the project. If those metrics aren't readily available already, you need to make sure that you start gathering those metrics as part of the project. Ideally, you'll want to do that first so that you can establish a baseline to compare against.

At the end of your project, you should think about the people that you worked closely with. Especially if there is anyone with whom you don't normally collaborate, you should consider having your manager ask them for feedback on your work on the project. I suggest this because people are really susceptible to the recency bias, a cognitive bias that tells us that people favors recent events over those further in the past. So if you work on a project with someone and then you ask them for feedback a year later when you're trying to get promoted, you'll often hear something like "Oh, I haven't worked with her in a long time. I don't know what I could add." By asking for feedback right at the end of a project, you'll likely get something far more substantial.

Last, and most importantly, you want to write all of this down somewhere. In chapter 5, we talked about keeping a work log. I would keep this information there AND in a separate document specifically detailing your impact toward your next promotion. By storing all of this information in an easy-to-find place, demonstrating your impact later on should become simple. Otherwise, you'll be stuck trying to remember what projects you worked on, let alone what impact you had and what metrics best showed that impact.

WHEN SHOULD YOU START PLANNING FOR PROMOTION?

From day one! The biggest mistake I see junior developers make is assuming that they need to wait until their manager tells them that they're ready for a promotion before they begin preparing for one. While your manager probably will, eventually, bring it up, it's going to take longer than if you're driving the process yourself. Why? Because promotions are all about showing your impact. You not only need to be *operating* at the next level, you must have data and evidence showing that. And as we just talked about above, it's easiest to collect this data starting from day one, while you're working on projects. And if you're not already thinking about your next promotion, you're not likely thinking about what data to grab and what metrics to highlight in order to show your impact.

Deciding that you want to work toward a promotion is also a great way of focusing your efforts. Since there are usually clear-cut responsibilities for engineers at each level, it makes it easy to focus on doing those things that will take you to the next one. Like the quote from Tara Jaye Frank says at the beginning of this chapter, don't get caught in the trap of assuming that just doing your job well will be enough to get a promotion. That's generally not the case at junior levels and it's *definitely* not the case at senior levels. Learning how to plan for a promotion is a skill that you can and should learn.

WHAT IF YOU DON'T GET PROMOTED?

This is a tough one. Being told your promotion didn't go through can be crushing and breaking that news to someone is honestly one of the hardest conversations you have to handle as a manager. If you've been following along so far, you can rest assured that:

1. Your manager did everything they could to advocate for you
2. You and your manager put together the strongest case possible
3. You've come out of the process with a concrete understanding of what gaps remain between where you are now and what's needed to achieve the next level.

Focusing on the third point, I firmly believe it is always better to try for a promotion and be told you're not ready than it is to sit back and wonder whether you're ready. Best case scenario, you get the promotion! Worst case, you get valuable information about your opportunity areas. This is why you should always make sure that your manager tells you exactly what you're missing.

It might feel like a sad consolation prize, but don't dismiss how important this learning is in the grand scheme of your career. You've gained valuable clarity on what areas you should focus on. Use this information to work with your manager to set new goals and a new timeline for promotion.

RECAP

Hopefully by the time you're reading this recap, you're sipping some celebratory champagne for your promotion. But just for ease of recall (and thinking ahead to your next promotion), here is what we talked about:

Understanding the Promotions Process

If you want to have the best chance at getting promoted, you need to make sure that you understand the process inside and out. That means learning who makes the decisions, how often promotion decisions are made, and what information is needed in order to justify the promotion. Only then can you be sure that you're putting your best self forward to whoever is deciding on your promotion.

Demonstrating Impact

For each project that you work on, it's important to think about what the impact will be and how you can measure it from the beginning. Whatever metrics you choose, make sure that you write them down somewhere you can easily find later. And don't forget to get written feedback from the people that you worked with at the end of the project rather than waiting until you're ready to get promoted, by which time they might have forgotten the specifics of working with you.

When Should You Start Planning for Promotion?

From the very start! If advancement is your goal, taking an active role in the promotions process will get you to the next level much faster than if you wait for your manager to decide that you're ready. Also, promotions make for great goals because they give you concrete things to focus on.

What If You Don't Get Promoted?

There's the elephant in the room. It's better to have tried and failed than to wonder if you could have gotten the promotion if you had only put yourself out there. If you find yourself in this unfortunate situation, the feedback that you get from the process will help you really make sure that you get it next time.

CHAPTER ELEVEN

When Is It Time for Something New?

"You've got to learn to leave the table when love's no longer being served."

— Nina Simone

You've made it to the last chapter. Congratulations! At this point, you've probably been at your company for a little while now. You might have even gotten a promotion or two. But whether you've been there for just a few months or several years, there comes a point when you start to wonder, *"When is it time for something new?"*

First, let's look at why you might be craving change.

REASONS FOR CHANGE

There are a million different reasons why you could be looking for a new opportunity, and all of them are valid. Here are a few common ones:

Looking to Learn Something New

Maybe you've spent too much time working eCommerce features and you want to learn how a social media app works. Maybe you've been working on Android apps for a few years now and are looking to learn backend development. Or maybe you've been at a big company for your entire career and want to see what a startup is like.

Some people find what they love early on and do that for their entire careers. But most people switch around every few years, exploring new areas as they search for their passion or perfect fit. Especially at the beginning of your career, I would recommend trying out a few different companies and types of development to see what interests you most.

Toxic Environment

Are you dealing with a micromanager? Or coworkers that constantly undermines you? I've even seen managers and companies pit people against one another. While it's admirable to try to stick it out and change things for the better, you don't owe it to anyone to suffer in a toxic environment.

More Money

The best way to ensure that you're getting paid top dollar is to switch jobs every 2 years or so, according to the Atlanta Federal Reserve Bank's wage growth tracker, which uses data from the U.S. Bureau of Labor Statistics. It's really unfortunate that that's the case, but it's true. Definitely try seeing what your company can offer in terms of a raise, but whether you're trying to chase a top dollar gig or just trying to make sure that you're being paid fairly for your level, compensation is a perfectly valid reason to think about switching jobs.

Better Work/Life Balance

Different companies view work/life balance differently. At big companies, even different orgs or teams can have different views on work/life balance. If your company thinks that you should be putting in 50, 60, or even 70-hour weeks, it could be time to start looking for a company that believes that we only have so many productive hours in the day. It could also be the PTO policy or culture that makes you consider leaving. Does the company give people very little time off, or make them feel guilty about taking it? Those are signs of a bad PTO culture.

Culture

Speaking of culture, the overall culture of a company can be a reason why you might want to leave. Maybe they don't do a great job of being inclusive of everyone. Or maybe they don't have any safe spaces for groups of non-stereotypical engineers to be able to take a break and be themselves. Or maybe they embody the "move fast and break things" philosophy a little *too* hard. Whatever it is, make sure that the next company has a culture that matches you, your beliefs, and your needs.

Lack of Diversity

A ton of companies have some sort of diversity and inclusion initiatives going on, but not all of them are very successful or taken very seriously. It can be really stressful and awkward to be the only woman on the team. Or the only Black person. Or the only disabled person. If your company isn't doing a good job of hiring more people who embody all different cultures, ethnicities, and abilities, it might be time to look for a company that takes diversity more seriously.

Wanting to Play a Bigger Role

It could be that you're ready to take on more responsibilities. Perhaps you're a senior engineer that wants to take on managerial responsibilities, but your path at your current job is blocked by the fact that your team already has a manager. I've definitely been in situations where it feels like I've been bumping up against my manager and have actually had to work out how to "officially" take over those responsibilities that I was basically doing already. Sometimes that's possible. Sometimes it's not, in which case you may find yourself looking for an opportunity on another team or at a different company.

Moving

This is a less common reason for switching jobs in this day and age (especially post-pandemic with so many companies supporting remote workers), but it's still something to consider. You might want to move to be closer to your family, for a lower cost of living, a change of scenery, or to experience something new. Especially if you usually work in an office, you're going to want to think about whether you can handle working remotely if you're moving to a different city, if that's even an option. Moving to a different country can also be a reason to consider changing jobs. Not all companies are able to hire or support employees internationally. And even if they are, it's important to think about things like time zone differences as you make these decisions.

LOOKING FOR NEW OPPORTUNITIES

Whatever your reasons for wanting to leave a team or a company, you have to learn how to discreetly find a new opportunity that is better than your current one. Two Steps Forward, No Steps Back

Before you get as far as interviewing or talking to recruiters about different opportunities, how do you make sure that a new company you're considering is actually an improvement over your current company? This is especially key if you're leaving a job because of an unhealthy or unfulfilling work environment.

You might want to brush up on chapters one and two again. The same practices of brainstorming what you were looking for, networking, and researching can help you here. The only difference is that now you know more about what you do and don't want in a team, a manager, and a company.

Speaking of networking, send out feelers in your network (yes, it's still important to have a network of engineers) to see if anyone works at the company you're considering or has worked there recently. It can be a good idea to get an insider's perspective on how the company operates and the culture you'll encounter there.

Searching Discreetly

You don't want your manager to know that you're looking for a new job, especially at the beginning of your search. So how do you let companies know that you're looking without tipping off your manager or your own company's recruiters? Tools like LinkedIn, Indeed, Hired, and other similar sites all have ways of letting recruiters know that you're open to new opportunities. Even better, they usually have an option to hide that status from people at your current company.

You can also search through a company's job postings and apply directly for positions that you're interested in, work with an agency, or reach out to recruiters directly.

There's Nothing Wrong About Interviewing

Society makes us think that we're disloyal if we interview at other companies while we're working. But the truth is, there is nothing wrong about interviewing. In fact, some people even do it on a regular basis just to keep their skills sharp. If your manager or company has a problem with that, then they should actually be afraid that they're not doing enough to make you *want* to stay. That being said, it can lead to some awkward conversations, and there are definite benefits to keeping it under wraps for as long as you can.

Balancing Interviewing and Working

The earlier stages of interviewing are easy to balance because they're usually just hour-long sessions and can conceivably be scheduled during lunch, right before work, or right after. The real difficulty comes when you're doing final round interviews. These usually take several hours if not a full day, so you pretty much have to take the day off. If you're only planning on interviewing at one or two companies, you could probably get away with taking a day off here and there. But if you're interviewing at several, you might want to plan to take a whole week off and schedule all of your interviews within that block.

Whatever you do, don't say that you're going to be working, even if it's remotely, and then actually go interview somewhere else. People can usually tell.

Can I Tell My Manager?

Is all the sneaking around really necessary? You *can* tell your manager that you're looking around, but I highly recommend that you don't. Unless you trust your manager to be able to handle it responsibly. I left my first job in Seattle because I decided that I wanted to move back to the Boston area. So I started looking for opportunities there, and I decided to give my manager ample notice that I was doing that. A few months later, I had lined up my new job and put in my notice. I timed my exit perfectly so that I would be eligible for my full performance bonus from the year prior. What I hadn't counted on, however, was that because I gave my manager so much of a heads up, he decided to reallocate my bonus to the rest of the team, leaving me with the grand total of $0. For those playing at home, that would be a 0% bonus.

Would every manager do this? Probably not — I sincerely hope not. But it is something to consider. We'll talk next about when and how you should tell your manager you are leaving.

TELLING YOUR MANAGER

Timing is everything. It can make the difference between leaving the company on a good note or a sour one. Or even losing out on money, if your manager is particularly lousy.

When Should I Tell My Manager?

In general, I'd recommend waiting until you've dotted your I's and crossed your T's before giving your manager notice. If you tell them too early, it tends to make things awkward. In my opinion, the sweet spot is between 2 and 4 weeks before you leave. It depends a lot on how much knowledge needs to be transferred and how many projects need to be re-assigned to leave the team in a healthy spot.

But in the end, especially if you're in a situation that's toxic or abusive, you shouldn't feel bad about just giving the minimum required 2 weeks' notice. Yes, it's nice if you can help the team prepare for your departure, but that comes second to your safety and well-being.

How Do I Tell Them I'm Leaving?

Telling your manager that you're leaving, whether you have a good relationship with them or not, can be a tough conversation. I would recommend telling your manager in person, during a regularly scheduled 1:1. Email and Slack aren't great mediums for tone and context. And whatever you do, please don't throw time on your manager's calendar with some generic description. We usually know when something is up, and it just makes things awkward and anxiety-inducing.

If you're unsure of what to say, here is a basic script you can use:

> *"I just wanted to let you know that I've been offered a role at another company [You can name the company, but you don't have to]. I've decided to accept that offer, and my last day will be on ___. Until then, I'm happy to help ensure that the transition is as smooth as possible. I'll send you an email with all of these details as my formal resignation notice."*

I think that's the most bare-bones you can make things. And honestly, unless you really love your manager, short and sweet is the way to go. Inviting them to ask questions can just make things uncomfortable for everyone. The last sentence is important, because they'll often need some sort of written notice of your resignation. It also serves as proof that you've had this conversation.

If telling your manager during something like a 1:1, I highly recommend trying to lead with this information. Otherwise, you'll spend the entire time worrying about it and trying to find a good time to bring it up. There is no good time; the only right time is now.

RECAP

At some point in everyone's career, there comes a time for something new. Here's how to go about chasing new opportunities and navigating that transition:

Reasons for Change

Whether you're looking to try something new, trying to get away from a toxic environment, moving to a new city, want more money, or want to play a bigger role, these are all valid reasons to look for your next opportunity.

Looking for New Opportunities

As you consider new companies and teams, make sure that your new opportunity is actually everything you hope it will be. There is nothing wrong or shameful about looking or interviewing around, though you may way to go about it discreetly and try to balance interviewing and your day job in a way that doesn't make it obvious you are on your way out.

Telling Your Manager

Timing is everything when it comes to notifying your manager. It's best to bring it up during a regularly scheduled meeting, like a 1:1. Try to get it out at the beginning of the meeting, because otherwise you're going to spend the entire time worrying about it. To make it as quick and painless as possible, you can use the script I provided.

Conclusion

You made it to the end. Give yourself a big pat on the back. That itself is a huge accomplishment! My hope is that you found at least some of the advice in this book useful and that you're able to learn from my experiences, including my mistakes. That's not to say that you'll never make mistakes of your own, but hopefully they'll be new and interesting ones to learn from rather than my boring old ones.

And don't forget: Anyone can make it in tech, if they're willing to put in the work. It doesn't matter if you're old or young. It doesn't matter if you've got a PhD in computer science, a Bachelor's degree in an unrelated field, or no degree at all. It doesn't matter if you're switching careers. It doesn't matter if you're Black, Latinx, Indigenous, trans, disabled, or anything else. You can learn how to develop software and you can make money doing it. If you take away only one thing from this book, let it be that **you** are the driver of your own career.

I recommend that you keep this book on your desktop, whether it's a physical desktop or a metaphorical one, and use it as a reference throughout your career. When you hit a new milestone in your career or if you're looking for quick refresher on something, the recaps are designed for exactly that.

No matter at what stage you are in your career, I thank you for going on this journey with me and I wish you the very best. I can't wait to see what you accomplish! Feel free to reach out to me on Twitter (@AutisticManager) — I'd love to hear from you.

— Alex

Appendix

TECHNICAL INTERVIEWING RESOURCES

De-Coding the Technical Interview Process
Emma Bostian, https://technicalinterviews.dev

Cracking the Coding Interview
Gayle Laakmann McDowell,
https://crackingthecodinginterview.com

The Algorithm Design Manual
Steven S. Skiena, https://thealgorist.com

UNDERSTANDING YOUR OFFER RESOURCES

Essential Options Trading Guide
https://www.investopedia.com/options-basics-tutorial-4583012

NEGOTIATION RESOURCES

Getting to Yes: Negotiating Agreement Without Giving In
William Ury, https://www.williamury.com/books/getting-to-yes/

Never Split the Difference
Chriss Voss, https://info.blackswanltd.com/never-split-the-difference

PAID MENTORSHIP/COACHING RESOURCES

MentorCruise
https://mentorcruise.com

FEEDBACK RESOURCES

Thanks for the Feedback: The Science and Art of Receiving Feedback Well
Douglas Stone & Sheila Heen,
https://www.stoneandheen.com/thanks-feedback

Radical Candor
Kim Scott, https://radicalcandor.com

Difficult Conversations: How to Discuss What Matters Most
Douglas Stone, Bruce Patton, & Sheila Heen,
https://www.stoneandheen.com/difficult-conversations

BOOK CLUB RESOURCES

Thanks for the Feedback: The Science and Art of Receiving Feedback Well
Douglas Stone & Sheila Heen,
https://www.stoneandheen.com/thanks-feedback

Radical Candor
Kim Scott, https://radicalcandor.com

Difficult Conversations: How to Discuss What Matters Most
Douglas Stone, Bruce Patton, & Sheila Heen,
https://www.stoneandheen.com/difficult-conversations

The Bootcamper's Companion
Caitlyn Greffly, https://www.bootcamperscompanion.com

The Manager's Path: A Guide for Tech Leaders Navigating Growth & Change
Camile Fournier

The Culture Code: Unlock the Secrets of Highly Successful Groups
Daniel Coyle, https://danielcoyle.com/the-culture-code/